Grand Slam Leadership

Using Baseball Principles and Strategies to Win in Business and Life

Dr. Bobby Olszewski

Winter Garden, FL

Grand Slam Leadership
Using Baseball Principles and Strategies to Win in Business and Life

Published by Emerson Management & Consulting Group, Inc.
Winter Garden, Florida

Printed in the United States of America
First Edition: January 2026

Hardcover ISBN: 979-8-9943431-0-4
Paperback ISBN: 979-8-9943431-1-1

Cover design by Felipe Samir
Photography by Mike Wacht

For information, permissions, or bulk orders, please contact: DrBobbyO@EmersonMCG.com

Legal Disclaimer

This book is an independent work of authorship. It is not sponsored by, endorsed by, approved by, or in any way affiliated with Major League Baseball, the Office of the Commissioner of Baseball, the Major League Baseball Players Association, or any professional sports league, team, player, coach, or organization.

All references to individuals, players, managers, teams, leagues, movies, characters, and organizations in and out of baseball are used solely for illustrative, educational, and informational purposes. Any names, likenesses, statistics, or other identifying features are used in a descriptive manner consistent with fair use principles under applicable intellectual property laws.

The views, interpretations, and opinions expressed herein are solely those of the author and do not necessarily reflect the views, opinions, or positions of any individual, organization, or entity referenced or acknowledged within this work.

Grand Slam Leadership Summary

Lead with Clarity, Play with Purpose, and Win with Integrity

Baseball has a simple way of bringing us back to what works. The game's timeless lessons of patience, fundamentals, teamwork, and resilience have guided us for generations. These principles still hold true in today's unpredictable times. When the world changes the rules, expectations rise, and the pressure to perform never stops. Baseball's fundamentals remind us how to slow things down, trust our instincts, and play with purpose.

In *Grand Slam Leadership*, Dr. Bobby Olszewski draws on three decades of leadership experience in business, communications, and public service to share 55 concise, powerful lessons that connect the ballpark to your workplace. Whether you are just launching your career or leading at the top of your organization, this book is your game plan for confidence and lasting results in business and life.

About the Author

Dr. Bobby Olszewski is a communications expert, educator, and public servant whose career has been shaped by transformational leadership, strategic messaging, and a commitment to helping organizations thrive. He has advised executives, coached teams, strengthened organizational cultures, and guided leaders in the public and private sectors through high-stakes communication challenges. His work includes leading successful campaigns that increased nonprofit revenue and conducting extensive research on donor motivations.

For more than twenty years, he has served as an adjunct professor, teaching students and professionals how to lead with clarity, purpose, and integrity. As a former State Representative in Florida, he represented the district that included the Walt Disney World Resort, Universal Orlando Resort, Sea World, and the Orange County Convention Center.

A lifelong baseball fan, Dr. Olszewski blends his academic and professional expertise with lessons from America's pastime to create a distinctive leadership philosophy grounded in discipline, teamwork, communication, and character. His book *Grand Slam Leadership* transforms baseball strategies into practical tools that help leaders at every level win the right way.

He holds a PhD in Business Administration, an MS in Management, an MA in Corporate Communication and Technology, and an undergraduate double major in Radio/Television and Organizational Communication. A devoted Cleveland Indians/Guardians fan, he lives in Orange County Florida with his wife and daughter and continues to believe in the dream of bringing Major League Baseball to Orlando.

Dedications and Acknowledgements

To my wife, Allison, and my daughter, Reagan, my heart belongs to you. I love you more than words could ever capture. Your love, encouragement, and patience, especially through watching countless baseball games, made this dream possible. This book is as much yours as it is mine.

To my parents, Bob and Rosie, thank you for giving me gifts of faith, family, and baseball. From Little League through life, you've been in the stands for every game. Dad, even though you left us much too soon, I live each day striving to make you and mom proud. I love you both more than I can ever repay.

My sincere gratitude and appreciation to Major League Baseball legends Barry Larkin, Johnny Damon, and AJ Pierzynski for their endorsement of this book.

A special thank you to Felipe Samir for this book's cover design and Mike Wacht for the photography.

Glory be to the Father, and to the Son, and to the Holy Spirit, as it was in the beginning, is now, and ever shall be, world without end. Amen.

⚾ Table of Contents ⚾

Theme: Lead yourself first by showing up with purpose, poise, and strategy.

This section is about owning your professional character. Just as great players step into the batter's box with a plan, successful professionals lead with focus, preparation, and intentionality. These chapters emphasize discipline, self-awareness, strategic thinking, and personal growth as foundational tools for effective leadership.

Core Topics: Focused decision-making, empowerment and trust, culture building, learning agility, knowing when to lead to let others shine.

Section 2: Collaboration

Together for the Win – Culture, Communication, and Teamwork

Theme: Teams win when trust, systems, and strategy all work together.

This section explores how strong team cultures and internal dynamics shape long-term performance. From launch strategies to team communication, it shows how thoughtful collaboration, alignment, and shared values can turn a group of individuals into a high-performing organization.

Core Topics: Team cohesion, communication and transparency, decision-making flexibility, cross-functional coordination, strategic alignment.

Section 3: Adaptability

Executing the Game Plan – *Strategic Flexibility with Situational Awareness*

Theme: Adjust your strategy based on the opportunity in the moment, not just because it's in the playbook.

This section focuses on real-time leadership, strategic execution, and adapting to changing conditions. Great teams make smart plays because they are situationally aware. These chapters guide professionals through decision-making that takes context, readiness, and momentum into account.

Core Topics: Situational strategy, resource alignment, talent development, resilience, agility under pressure, sustaining momentum.

Section 4: Precision

Delivering in the Moment *– Clear Communication & Alignment Under Pressure*

Theme: Providing clarity under pressure builds trust and credibility.

When the stakes are high, how you communicate defines your leadership. This section equips professionals with tools to manage difficult conversations, align messaging, and lead through high-visibility moments. Like clutch performers on the field, communicators win when they stay composed and precise.

Core Topics: Message discipline, alignment, crisis response, transparency, audience adaptation.

Section 5: Legacy

Beyond the Game – *Purpose, Impact, & Influence Beyond the Field*

Theme: Build something that lasts by leading with meaning, not just the metrics.

This final section focuses on long-term influence. It challenges professionals to connect their work to greater purpose, create meaningful narratives, and build loyalty. Just as the most loved players are remembered for how they made people feel, leaders and brands leave lasting impact when they stand for something deeper.

Core Topics: Purpose-driven storytelling, loyalty, narrative clarity, navigating disruption, visionary leadership.

⚾ Introduction⚾

"The one constant through all the years, has been baseball."

Terrance Mann - *Field of Dreams*

Simple, Proven, and Effective - Baseball's Blueprint for Your Success

Think back to your earliest memory of baseball.

It might have been a hot summer afternoon at the ballpark, where the smell of peanuts and the crack of the bat created a stillness that made everything in life feel right. Maybe it was a ball game playing quietly on your grandfather's radio, voices rising with excitement because of a double in the gap. Perhaps it was you, standing on a Little League diamond, waiting for your turn at bat, nervously glancing at your parents in the stands.

Whatever solidified your first connection to baseball, it involved more than the rules of the game. It involved people and the stories they created. Family and moments, filled with both serenity and celebration. Baseball has always offered a gentle rhythm that feels reassuring, especially when the world beyond the outfield fence feels out of control.

That balance is still with us today.

For over 160 years, baseball has been a constant presence across generations. Our parents, grandparents, great-grandparents, and even our great-great-grandparents shared this game. The players have changed, the rules have evolved, but the soul of baseball remains untouched. In a world where so much feels uncertain, the game has never lost its way.

Today, we are all navigating a workplace in an environment that seems to change faster than we can keep up. Artificial intelligence, hybrid work models, shifting cultural norms, economic volatility, and the constant pressure to perform have created an office where many professionals feel like they are playing an evolving game without a rulebook.

For many, the modern business world has changed the rules and established professional norms out of thin air. Expectations shift daily. Attention spans are shorter. Concepts are measured in 280 characters or less and even a ten second video reel can be too long with society's diminishing focus. Clarity is rare, and chaos seems to be the new normal. Just when we think we have figured it out, the strike zone seems to change on us again.

Grand Slam Leadership offers you a refreshing sense of tranquility through a game we all love. A game that thrives in complexity, teaches through failure, rewards consistency, and reveals character in pressure. That game is our game, and that game is baseball.

More than a sport, baseball is a guidebook for how to lead, how to grow, how to adapt, and how to stay grounded. The same principles that apply to the diamond also apply in the boardroom, on the Zoom call, the performance review, and in the press conference. You do not need to be a former player or a lifelong fan to understand these concepts. You just need to slow down long enough to recognize the timeless wisdom the game has always offered.

Baseball is not complicated. It is strategic, but at its core, the game has always been honest. It is about teamwork and preparation. It is a child's game played by grown-ups under bright lights. In that simple truth lies its power. Baseball reminds us that even in the complexity of this day and age, we can still rely on what works.

We can still trust patience.
We can still value fundamentals.
We can still believe in the team.
We can still come back after failure.

This book shares 55 chapters, each one a leadership lesson drawn from our nation's pastime and applied to the life of business. You will learn how to build your bullpen, so you are never caught alone on the mound. You will see how internal culture wins games before you ever take the field. You will discover how to watch the signals, trust the scoreboard, and know when it is time to take a pitch instead of swinging for the fences.

Most importantly, you will learn how to find meaning and peace in your career, your team, and in your leadership journey. Not by inventing new rules, but by remembering the old ones that still hold true, which we simply have forgotten. Baseball will serve as your metaphor, your mirror, and your mentor.

I have brought to this book more than three decades of experience in business, public service, leadership, marketing, and communication. I have led teams, built strategies, served the public as an elected official, managed crises, taught students, and mentored professionals. Through it all, I have seen the same challenges resurface. The lack of simplicity, pressure to conform, confusion in times of change, and a longing for something to make it all make sense again.

What is missing is not that latest technological upgrade, social media post notification, or more advice about becoming an influencer. It is a return to the ballpark. Baseball offers what the modern workplace has forgotten. Simplicity with trust, repetition, accountability, grace under pressure, and the understanding that one at-bat does not define your season.

If you are a college student trying to find your swing, or a seasoned executive trying to lead in a world that no longer plays by the rules you were taught, this book will give you the insights you need to achieve success. These pages are for anyone who wants to communicate more clearly, lead more confidently, market more authentically, and, most importantly, live more intentionally.

These pages are for professionals who want to win, not just at work, but win with integrity in all areas of life. You may never hit a home run in Yankee Stadium, but you have your own ballpark to play. Your team. Your game. Your season. You are not just a player. You are a coach, a communicator, a strategist, and a teammate.

Get your seat in the dugout. Dust off your glove. Open your heart to the lessons you already know and let the game bring you back to the fundamentals that still work in business, in leadership, and in life. Just like in the game of baseball, you must be ready for the pitch to hit in your sweet spot.

The one constant, the one that still holds true, the one that is still calling to us when we feel lost or overwhelmed, is baseball.

Let's play ball!

Dr. Bobby Olszewski
Servant Leader, Communications Strategist, and Business Educator

⚾ Hall of Fame Tribute to My Childhood Hero and All-Time Favorite Player ⚾

Gary Carter

Living with Joy, Leading with Purpose, and Catching Life with Both Hands

Baseball Principle

Gary Carter was more than a Hall of Fame catcher. He was the heartbeat of every team he played on from the Montreal Expos, New York Mets, San Francisco Giants, to his hometown Los Angeles Dodgers. He was the kind of player who combined fierce competitiveness with an unshakable optimism and exuberance. Nicknamed "The Kid" for his youthful energy and infectious smile, Gary brought passion to every play, every inning, and every game he entered. His numbers alone are remarkable being a ten-time All-Star and a two-time All-Star game MVP, winning three Gold Gloves and five Silver Slugger awards, and was a cornerstone of the 1986 World Series Champion Mets. Carter even won the Roberto Clemente Award for his outstanding character and community service off the field.

The real story of Gary Carter lives beyond the statistics and accolades. He was a leader behind the plate, in the locker room, and with the fans. He called games with precision, handled his pitching staff with care, and lifted his teammates through encouragement, not ego. As a catcher, he played the toughest position in baseball and never took a day off mentally or emotionally. He believed in doing things the right way, every day, without shortcuts or excuses. Whether it was a pennant race or a midseason slump, Gary Carter showed up ready to serve his team, honoring his character, family, and faith.

Business Strategy

In many ways, Gary Carter represents the kind of leadership every organization needs today. The kind of leadership that blends skill with sincerity, ambition with authenticity, and success with unwavering service. Known for his boundless energy and genuine optimism, Carter led not by command but by connection. He inspired through consistency, preparation, and an unwavering belief that leadership was about elevating others, not himself.

Carter's leadership style translates powerfully to the modern workplace. In an era where teams are often spread across time zones, where burnout runs high, and where trust is fragile, his approach offers a blueprint. He didn't just perform but also built relationships with his teammates. He checked in with his pitchers before every game, not just about mechanics, but about mindset. He lifted teammates who were struggling and gave credit freely when others succeeded. He showed that encouragement and accountability can coexist, and that optimism, when rooted in purpose, is a performance strategy, not a personality trait.

Imagine applying the same leadership in today's corporate environment. A project manager, who starts every meeting by asking how their team is really doing. A CEO who takes time to walk the floor, thank employees by name, and celebrate small wins. A department leader who stays late to mentor a new hire or responds to criticism with calm and care instead of defensiveness. Those small acts of steady, grounded leadership ripple outward, creating cultures where people feel seen, supported, and motivated to give their best.

For business professionals, Gary Carter's legacy is a reminder that greatness is not measured in titles or metrics, but in trust. It's not only what you achieve, but how you achieve it. Leadership is how you treat people, how you respond under pressure, and how you turn every day into an opportunity to lead with joy, humility, and heart.

Real-World Example

Gary Carter's story embodies the kind of leadership that stands the test of time. Leadership that is steady under pressure, joyful in the grind, and anchored by purpose. In today's business world, his example mirrors the leaders who carry the heaviest loads not for recognition, but for responsibility. These are the leaders who mentor emerging talent after back-to-back meetings, the department heads who take ownership of challenges rather than assigning blame, and the executives who remember every name in the hallway and every story behind the work.

Consider a senior vice president at a fast-growing company who was handed an impossible assignment in leading a company-wide restructuring while keeping morale intact. The pressure was relentless. Layoffs loomed. Teams were uncertain. Instead of hiding behind memos or metrics, this leader met with every department personally. They listened more than they spoke, answered questions directly, and focused every conversation on respect and rebuilding. They sent handwritten thank-you notes to those transitioning out and offered references and networking connections to help them land on their feet.

Months later, when the dust settled, the company had stabilized. Productivity rose, turnover dropped, and employee trust remarkably increased. People routinely said the same thing, the leader cared enough to show up. That is the Gary Carter effect. Leading with humility, presence, and compassion even when the moment calls for toughness.

Like Carter, these leaders understand that true influence comes not from position, but from presence. It's found in how you listen, how you lift others, and how you lead when the cameras are off. He lived his values in every inning and every interaction, reminding us that real greatness is about how faithfully you serve.

Gary Carter was a devoted husband, a loving father, and a man of deep Christian faith who never separated who he was off the field from who he was on it. Even in his last battle with brain cancer, Carter remained hopeful, inspiring, and focused on others. His joy and light never dimmed. His faith never broke no matter the pressures he was facing against all odds up until the very end surrounded by his family.

Business Tip

To lead like Gary Carter, bring these lessons into your professional life:

- Show up every day with joy and discipline, no matter how hard work becomes
- Put the team first, always offering support, encouragement, and service
- Let your faith or guiding principles ground your decisions and shape your character
- Play with heart, even when the spotlight is not on you

Leadership is not commanding attention because of a title. It is about being present and dependable. It's doing things the right way and building influence that lasts.

Final Thought

Gary Carter was more than my favorite baseball player. He was the reason I fell in love with the game. He was the player I wanted to emulate, not just for how he played, but for how he lived his life. His legacy starts this book because he embodied everything great leadership stands to deliver. He won with integrity, faith, enthusiasm, and heart. He proved that you can be fierce without being ruthless, confident without being arrogant, and joyful without losing your competitive fire.

Every one of us has a Gary Carter somewhere in our story. A person who modeled what it means to lead with grace, to stand tall under pressure, and to make others better just by believing in them. For me, he was that light. For others, it might be a mentor, a teacher, a parent, a boss, or a coach. Whoever it is, their example reminds us that the greatest leaders are not remembered for what they won, but for how they made others feel.

Heroes like Gary Carter never truly leave us. Their words still speak to us. Their example endures. Their spirit lives on in everyone they inspired. The best way to honor them is to lead the same way with love, with courage, and with unwavering faith in what's right.

Thank you, Gary Carter, for inspiring me to lead with faith and heart. Catch you later, Kid.

⚾ Section 1: Discipline ⚾

1

Scout Before You Pitch – Stakeholder Research & Personalization

Mastering the Moment Through Preparation and Precision

Baseball Principle

Every great pitcher knows that success begins long before the first pitch. The game may be decided on the field, but championships are built in quiet moments of study, and in the endless pursuit of understanding the opponent. True advantage doesn't come from raw talent alone. It comes from insight, from preparation, and knowing exactly what to do when the moment arrives to perform.

Before each game, the clubhouse hums with focus. Scouting reports glow on tablets, filled with stats, spray charts, and coded notes from coaches. Pitchers become detectives, looking for tells on the batter who flinches at sliders low and away, the one who crowds the plate against fastballs inside, or the veteran who can't resist a changeup when behind in the count.

Few embodied this mastery better than Hall of Fame pitcher Greg Maddux. He didn't just pitch, he orchestrated. His genius was in his mind as much as his arm. In one famous regular-season game against the Astros, Maddux intentionally threw Jeff Bagwell a fastball that Bagwell launched over the fence in a calculated mistake. Months later, in the playoffs, with the game on the line, Bagwell stepped in expecting that same pitch. Maddux delivered a changeup away, freezing him for strike three. The move had been planned months earlier in a setup that only Maddux could see coming.

That's the power of true scouting. Turning knowledge into anticipation. The great pitchers don't play checkers. They play chess thinking three moves ahead of batter. They win by reading the field, knowing the patterns, and trusting the preparation that began long before the crowd ever arrived.

Scouting isn't busy work or guesswork but the blueprint of success. It's the discipline to study when no one's watching, the humility to prepare when others rely on instinct, and the courage to execute a plan built for that exact moment.

Business Strategy

Too many professionals walk into meetings armed with the same polished slides, the same talking points, and the same one-size-fits-all presentation. They deliver their message flawlessly but fail to make it meaningful because it doesn't reflect the person or organization sitting across the table. The words sound sharp, but the connection falls flat.

Great leaders understand that research is not just homework. It's a form of respect. Taking the time to learn about your audience, their goals, their pain points, and even their language, transforms communication from a performance into a partnership. When you show that you've done the work to understand them, you demonstrate that their priorities matter as much as your own. That's when dialogue replaces presentation and real trust begins to form.

Stakeholder scouting extends far beyond sales. It's the foundation of leadership. Every person you interact with, from your CEO to your newest intern, has a different way of processing information, expressing emotion, and defining success. The best leaders learn to read those cues like pitchers reading batters. They know who needs a deep dive into data and who needs the big-picture vision, who thrives on recognition and who values quiet acknowledgment, who moves fast and who prefers reflection.

The most successful professionals don't rely on volume of their voice to get their message across. They rely on precision. They listen before they speak, prepare before they perform, and deliver with empathy and clarity. Because in leadership, as in pitching, success doesn't come from throwing everything you've got. It comes from knowing exactly what the person in front of you needs to hear and delivering it right on target.

Real-World Example

A firm was preparing to make a presentation to a public housing agency. Instead of using their standard slide deck, they spent several days reading the agency's five-year work plan, reviewing board meeting notes, and researching the organization's challenges.

When it came time to present, they opened by saying, "we know one of your current goals is improving multilingual engagement throughout the state. Here is what we accomplished on a similar project within overlapping communities."

The tone shifted immediately. It was not a sales presentation anymore. It was a partnership conversation. That agency eventually became a long-term client, and the firm credited their research and preparation for sealing the deal.

Business Tip

Know the situation through scouting the stakeholders in your professional environment:

- Create a scouting report before every high-stakes meeting
- Speak in terms of their goals, their mission, and their measures of success and tailor your communication to reflect their language, not yours
- Practice active curiosity in their daily interactions to learn what they care about
- Pay attention to how stakeholders react, what they prioritize, and how they communicate

You are not just showing what you know. You are showing that you care enough to prepare.

Final Thought

Success in any field is not defined by raw talent alone. It's defined by readiness. Greg Maddux didn't dominate because he threw the hardest fastball. He dominated because he understood his opponents better than anyone else. His brilliance came not from power, but from preparation. He studied, anticipated, and executed with perfect precision his location on each pitch he threw.

In business, preparation is your superpower. The time you invest in understanding people, organizations, and environments always pays you back. Often happening when the stakes are at their highest. When you walk into a meeting, an interview, or a negotiation, remember that the real work was done long before you entered the room. You win not by improvising, but by anticipating and executing a strategy.

Don't think of scouting as motion instead of progressive action. It's groundwork that transforms effort into execution. When you take the time to learn the people across from you, understand the conditions you're operating in, and tailor your strategy to the moment, you turn uncertainty into confidence. You start placing the ball exactly where it needs to be.

Know where the glove is set up for your target. Trust the plan. Anticipate every pitch and every decision with intention. The smartest leaders aren't lucky, because they're ready. They are prepared professionals who gather enough insight that guessing becomes unnecessary. In the end, the difference between a strikeout and a walk-off hit often comes down to whether you choose to throw blindly or throw with purpose.

2

Don't Swing at Every Pitch – Strategic Focus & Time Management

Success Comes from Patient Selectivity

Baseball Principle

Success in baseball often comes down to what a player doesn't swing at. Plate discipline is what separates good hitters from great ones. Legends like Ted Williams and Tony Gwynn built their careers not just on hand-eye coordination, but on patience, precision, and trust in their plan. They didn't waste energy chasing bad pitches or swinging out of frustration. They knew the count, studied the pitcher, and waited for the one pitch they could drive.

Ted Williams once said that the most important skill a hitter could develop was knowing the strike zone better than the umpire. That wasn't arrogance but situational awareness. Williams understood that discipline created opportunity. Every borderline pitch he let go was an act of control. He wasn't waiting passively but hunting selectively.

This kind of patience is power. Every swing takes energy, every chase creates risk, and every decision determines the outcome. The great hitters don't panic when the perfect pitch doesn't come right away. They stay calm, stay focused, and trust their preparation. Success is about waiting for the right opportunity and being ready to deliver when it arrives.

Business Strategy

Modern professionals face the same pressure at the office every day. The inbox fills, the meetings multiply, and every request feels urgent. The temptation is to swing at all of it, to say yes, to take on every project, to answer every call while believing that effort equals progress. Just like in baseball, swinging wildly leads to exhaustion, not excellence.

The best business leaders do not chase everything. They evaluate each pitch as a new opportunity. They recognize when a meeting is not worth their presence, when a task falls outside their priority zone, and when a new opportunity does not align with their mission.

They understand that busyness is not the same as productivity. By being selective with their swings, they protect their energy for the moments that matter most. Strategic focus is not laziness. It's leadership. It's having the courage to let good opportunities go so you can fully deliver on the great ones.

Real-World Example

A sales director had built a reputation for doing everything. Every client request, every last-minute proposal, every customization, they took it all on personally. Custom proposals, last-minute travel, and endless follow-ups. It wore them out and made their team frantic. Their performance looked busy but was not connected with the clients or their team.

Following strategic coaching sessions, the sales director implemented a filter system to evaluate new tasks. Each task had to meet three criteria. These benchmarks include alignment with quarterly goals, relevance to a client with long-term value, and whether it required the director's unique involvement.

The change was immediate when they applied the strategy. Stress dropped. Wins increased. Their personal reputation improved along with their team's results. They were no longer swinging at every pitch. They were picking their pitch and hitting it with power.

Business Tip

To build strategic discipline into your day, use these tools:

- Define your sweet spot by what you are best at and what your team needs most
- Know exactly where your skills and your mission overlap
- Reserve time for deep work and reflection by scheduling breathing room
- Practice saying no with confidence because every commitment should mean something

Success is not just about availability. It is about alignment.

Final Thought

One impatient swing at the wrong pitch can turn a rally into an inning-ending out. When you chase every opportunity, you spread your energy thin, lose your focus, and exhaust your team. The professionals who win, the true leaders, are the ones who have learned the confidence of patience.

They know when to wait. They know when to pass. When their moment finally comes, they swing with purpose, precision, and power.

Every career sees its share of pitches, some fast, some tempting, some meant to throw you off-balance. The difference between burnout and breakthrough is knowing which ones to ignore and which ones to crush.

Your success won't be defined by the number of swings you take. It will be defined by the moments you connect. When patient preparation meets opportunity, you send a line drive soaring into the gap because you waited for your pitch. That's not luck. That's discipline. That's mastery.

3

Your Bullpen Is Your Backbone – Delegation & Leadership Depth

Winning with Team Depth, Role Clarity, and Trust

Baseball Principle

The game's best starting pitchers rarely throw complete games. Even legends hand off the ball by the seventh or eighth inning. This is when the bullpen takes over with a fresh arm. A good bullpen is not just backup. It is part of a plan. It is a strategic decision made before the game even begins.

The bullpen is not just a safety net. It's a weapon. Managers build their pen with purpose with a mix of roles designed to protect the lead and close the deal. The setup man bridges the middle innings, keeping momentum alive. The closer enters under pressure, knowing the game's fate may rest on a single pitch. Every role is timed, defined, and trusted.

Championship teams understand this strategy. They know when to push and when to hand over the ball. The best managers make the call to the bullpen before fatigue turns into failure. That call represents one thing, trust. Trust that the team is built deep enough, strong enough, and ready enough to finish what was started.

No championship is ever won by a pitcher who refuses to let go. It's won by a team that knows how to carry each other across to victory. The bullpen is there to secure the win.

Business Strategy

Too many professionals try to be their company's entire pitching staff, the starter, the reliever, the closer, and sometimes even the umpire. They handle every decision, every detail, every crisis, believing that doing it all proves dedication. In truth, it only proves exhaustion and chaos.

Great leaders know that delegation is not about giving work away, it's about giving others the opportunity to lead. It's about trusting your bullpen to step in when the pressure builds and recognizing that success is not sustained by individual endurance but by collective strength.

When a leader delegates strategically, they're not just protecting their own time, they're multiplying capability. They're building leaders behind them. A well-developed team doesn't panic when the starter steps off the mound. They're ready because they've been trusted before the pressure hits.

Real-World Example

A creative director at a design firm was known for brilliance but also for burnout. The team admired their work but felt sidelined. The creative director reviewed everything, edited everything, and presented everything. It always had to be their idea.

Eventually, they realized their bullpen was full of unused talent. They assigned campaign ownership to the associate directors, moved weekly reviews into their hands, and encouraged them to present directly to clients. Allowing the team to become a team with key contributions ultimately produced results that benefited everyone.

Within three months, productivity doubled, morale soared, and they found time to focus on bigger strategy. The team did not fall apart. It grew stronger because they stopped being the entire rotation and started acting like a manager utilizing all the resources in their bullpen.

Business Tip

To build a reliable bullpen in your organization:

- Know who is best suited for what challenge
- One person should not carry the whole project for the entire team
- Delegate full roles and responsibility, not just simple tasks
- Practice handoffs during calm moments so your team is ready under pressure

A bullpen is not just made up of backups. It is made of difference-makers playing to win.

Final Thought

The greatest managers in baseball know that a tired arm can lose a game they've already won. The same is true in leadership. When you refuse to hand off responsibility, you rob others of the chance to grow. You also risk losing what you worked so hard to build.

Handing someone the ball is not letting go of control. Smart leaders know it's letting go of limitation. You tell your team we are going to protect what we've created together. That trust builds loyalty. It builds depth. It builds a team that performs long after the original leader steps off the mound.

One day, your bullpen will save the game. Another time, someone you've trained will deliver the final pitch that seals the victory. When that moment comes, it won't just be your win. It will be the team's win, because of your courage to trust them with the ball.

Great leaders don't throw every pitch in every inning. They build teams that can carry both the game and the legacy forward. Collectively earning victory for the team.

4

Coach from the Dugout – Empowerment & Servant Leadership

True Leadership Shines When Others Succeed

Baseball Principle

The manager never steps into the batter's box during the game. Once the lineup cards are exchanged, the game belongs to the players. A coach can call pitches, adjust the positioning on the field, or signal a hit and run, but the swing always belongs to the batter at the plate. The game is ultimately played by the team, not the person filling out the lineup card, and smart leaders are keenly aware of that fact.

Great managers can make all the difference. They observe. They coach. They inspire. They earn trust by first building trust. Their influence shows not in the volume of their voice but in the poise of their team. They lead from the dugout with the tone and trust they have already solidified and cultivated with their team.

Legendary managers like Joe Torre, Dusty Baker, and Bobby Cox were never known for fiery speeches or their ego-driven leadership. They were respected because they understood the people on their team and the game they played. They gave their players space to perform and support when it counted most.

Business Strategy

Leadership is not achieved in the spotlight. It is a platform you earn in the private moments. You do not build influence by being the strongest personality in the room. You build leadership by creating conditions where others can thrive by inspiring others to shine.

Micromanagement can feel like security to the leader, but it's pure suffocation to the team. Servant leadership takes the opposite approach. It asks, what do you need from me to do your best work and then let me get out of your way. The servant leader delivers what is needed without overshadowing the result.

Real leadership is found in quiet consistency. In setting vision, supporting execution, and knowing when to step in and when to step back. The best leaders do not chase credit. They celebrate team wins bolder than they would their own. They know that greatness is not what they do but what they build together with others.

Real-World Example

A director at a logistics firm was known for their calm presence and consistent results. They did not dominate meetings. They listened. They did not control projects. They clarified expectations and coached their teams. Their department consistently exceeded goals, not because they pushed harder, but because they built systems of support that empowered people to lead their own work.

When a junior project manager made a public error in a stakeholder meeting, they defended them without flinching. Afterward, the leader used the moment as a coaching opportunity, not to assign blame, but to reinforce growth. That junior project manager went on to lead some of the department's most critical initiatives. That is leadership without ego. That is coaching from the dugout empowering your team to perform on the field.

Business Tip

To lead with quiet strength by letting your team do the talking:

- Set clear expectations, then release control
- Offer feedback consistently, not just in formal reviews
- Support learning moments instead of punishing mistakes
- Make recognition routine and inclusive
- Ask more than you tell because the spotlight is not on you but your team

Your team does not need a superhero. They need a coach who believes in their talent and abilities, motivating them towards success.

Final Thought

You cannot step to plate for your team, but you can prepare them to face their moment in the batter's box with confidence. The real magic of leadership rarely happens under the stadium lights. It happens quietly in the dugout out of sight. Leaders have conversations that build trust well before the critical moments of the game. Effective leaders offer the guidance that shapes courage and pass on their belief in their team long before the first pitch is thrown.

There is nothing more rewarding than watching someone you have mentored step into their own moment and drive home the winning run. True leaders do not need their name on the scoreboard to feel victorious. Their greatest triumph is knowing they built the foundation, gave trust, and lit the spark that helped someone else succeed. Because in the end, the measure of a leader is not how many wins they claim, but how many wins they inspire. True leaders lead without needing applause because their greatest win is watching others succeed as the team achieves victory.

5

Manage the Clubhouse First – Internal Culture Drives External Results

You Cannot Win on the Field if You Are Losing the Locker Room

Baseball Principle

The game is more than just statistics and numbers on the scoreboard. Baseball is energy. It is chemistry. It is faith built between teammates who spend more than 200 days a year in a 162-game season together. When a team's clubhouse is united, the dugout feels alive. Players have each other's backs. Roles are understood. Egos stay in check. Winning becomes a shared purpose.

When the culture breaks down, so does everything else. Even the most talented rosters have underperformed when plagued by selfishness, poor communication, or fractured confidence. A bad clubhouse poisons performance throughout the team. A strong clubhouse elevates average players into champions.

Managers, like Terry Francona and Joe Maddon, who put their players first understand this by prioritizing the locker room as much as the scouting report. They know that unity off the field fuels execution on it. Their self-images are in check, which allows their teams to flourish by making it fun to come to work every day.

Business Strategy

The same principle applies in organizations. Your brand is only as strong as your culture. When employees feel heard, respected, and part of a team, they produce better work. When internal dynamics are toxic, it spills into client experiences, stakeholder relationships, and bottom-line outcomes.

Culture is not posters on a wall or in occasional catered lunches. It is routine behavior. It is how your team treats each other when no one is watching. It is the tone leaders set in meetings, in emails, in how they respond to pressure, are what truly lead to results.

Leaders who focus only on outward results without investing in internal belief often find themselves fixing problems they could have prevented. Culture is not a distraction from performance. It is the engine of culture, in which positive leaders regularly ignite the spark.

Real-World Example

An operations team in a travel tour business was struggling with turnover and missed deadlines. Leadership kept pushing for productivity and strong customer experience. More reports. More metrics. More pressure. But nothing improved the results.

A new director came in and took a different approach. In their first month they held listening sessions with every team member, documented internal challenges, and made three small but meaningful changes including improved internal communications, added recognition for behind-the-scenes work, and encouraged team lunches once a month.

The culture shift was impactful. People felt seen. Morale improved. The deadlines started getting hit without being chased. When the internal culture was fixed, the external performance followed. Customers noticed the difference with their results of exceptional tours as the company's revenue increased.

Business Tip

To manage your clubhouse like a seasoned professional:

- Prioritize internal communication with the same focus as external messaging
- Recognize small wins to build momentum and morale
- Address toxic behavior early before it shapes the culture
- Involve your team in shaping the values they want to live by
- Lead with consistency as your tone sets the tempo for everyone else

Culture is not a luxury. It is an essential leadership responsibility that starts at the top.

Final Thought

No one can perform at their best in a broken clubhouse. You can have the sharpest game plan, the latest technology, and a roster full of top talent. However, if the environment is toxic, everything slows, fractures, and eventually fails. A great team is not just motivated, it is aligned. It is built on a foundation where every player feels safe to speak up, supported when they stumble, and seen for the value they bring.

Manage your clubhouse as carefully as you manage your strategy. Build trust before you chase results. Because the way you treat your team behind closed doors will shape how they carry your message into the world. That is not just good leadership, it is the kind of legacy that endures long after the season is over. Years later, your team will not remember what you said, maybe not exactly what you accomplished together, but they will remember how you made them feel in the culture you created together.

6

Lead Off with Speed – First-Mover Advantage in Innovation

You Cannot Steal Second with Your Foot Still on First

Baseball Principle

The leadoff hitter in baseball is not just a fast baserunner. Their goal is to get on base where they are purposefully disruptive. Their job is to be the spark plug in the game from the very first pitch. By getting on base, applying pressure with speed, and forcing the defense to adjust, they give their team an early advantage.

Great leadoff hitters like Rickey Henderson, Ichiro Suzuki, and Kenny Lofton were not always the biggest names in the lineup, but they controlled momentum. A stolen base or a hustle double could set the tone for the entire game.

Speed creates opportunity but a disruptive strategy on the basepaths creates even more advantages. The first move forces the opponent to react. When the first move is bold and calculated, it opens the door to multiple runs on the scoreboard.

Business Strategy

The first mover advantage is the professional equivalent of a leadoff single. Companies that innovate early, adapt quickly, and launch tactically can seize market share before others even step to the plate.

Being first does not mean being reckless. It means recognizing opportunity, preparing with precision, and moving before hesitation turns into missed chances. It means identifying trends, reading the market, and acting while others are still planning.

The modern business environment rewards agility. Whether it is launching a new service, responding to public sentiment, or investing in emerging technology, those who lead off with speed often own the inning and eventually the game.

Real-World Example

A transit agency saw electric buses as a long-term growth strategy. Most peers were waiting on grants, policies, and public opinion to catch up. Their operations director saw the moment differently immediately made an impact when getting the agency on base.

They led the charge early, securing pilot funding, launching an education campaign, and branding the initiative before the first bus arrived. By the time other agencies joined the conversation, the agency had already earned media attention, secured additional support, and built public trust in the emerging technology. The agency did not wait for permission. They led off with the right vendor to ensure long term service and available parts in the emerging technology. They changed the game because they had the courage to get on base.

Business Tip

To create a first mover mindset like a true leadoff hitter:

- Watch the data but trust your instincts when momentum builds
- Empower small teams to test, learn, and adapt quickly
- Create clear approval paths so great ideas do not get stuck in review
- Use pilot projects as planned base hits that open the inning
- Communicate early wins to build confidence and secure buy-in

Innovation does not always come with a grand slam in the bottom of ninth inning. Sometimes it starts with a walk and a stolen base. When you get on base, make that first move and start the rally.

Final Thought

Raw speed means nothing without direction. The greatest leadoff hitters succeed not because they are the fastest, but because they are the most intentional. They read every move, the pitcher's cadence, the catcher's stance, the defense's attention, and when the moment comes, they react and go. Their success lies not in reaction, but in readiness.

Momentum is never accidental. It is earned through courage, timing, and trust in preparation. Those who hesitate watch opportunity slip away. Those who move with conviction, create it.

In leadership and in life, be the one who sets things in motion. Step forward before conditions are perfect. Lead with purpose, not permission. Because sometimes the entire rally, the comeback, the win itself, begins with one person willing to take the first step and run to ignite the spark.

7

Batting Practice Never Ends – Lifelong Learning & Team Development

Practice Is Not Preparation for the Game, It's Part of the Game

Baseball Principle

Even the most naturally gifted players in history treated batting practice as essential. Ken Griffey Jr., one of the smoothest and most beloved hitters the game has ever seen, never relied on talent alone. Fans remember the towering home runs, the effortless swing, and the highlight-reel catches, but what made him great was what happened before the stadium lights came on. Griffey was often the first to the cage, taking round after round of swings, refining timing, studying pitches, and sharpening his approach.

For Junior, batting practice was not a chore. It was part of the game itself. He knew that no matter how many homers he had already hit, the next at-bat would demand fresh focus and preparation. His swing may have looked effortless, but the truth was in the thousands of repetitions behind every fluid motion. The batting cage was where adjustments happened, where timing was restored, and where confidence was renewed.

Even for a Hall of Famer, the fundamentals never went away. They were revisited every day. Griffey's greatness was not only measured by his 630 career home runs. It was built in the countless unseen swings he took long before fans filled the stands.

Business Strategy

The most successful professionals are not the ones who arrive with all the answers. They are the ones who arrive ready to learn, adapt, and grow, every single day. They study the changing landscape of their industry. They seek mentors. They read widely, reflect deeply, and ask sharper questions today than they did yesterday.

Too often, organizations treat training like a box to check or a compliance requirement. But true development is not a one-time seminar or an annual retreat. It is ongoing growth throughout the organization. Lifelong learning is the batting practice of leadership and team success. Just as major leaguers step into the batting practice cage before every game, professionals at every level must keep sharpening their craft.

When organizations build development into their culture, they do more than add skills in their workforce. They create resilience, foster engagement, and instill confidence in their teams. Employees who feel invested in are more likely to invest back, with loyalty, creativity, and performance. Training becomes less about fixing weaknesses and more about reinforcing strengths, building momentum, and ensuring that when the pressure comes, the swing is second nature.

Real-World Example

An engineering firm had some of the brightest technical staff in its sector, yet its leadership noticed a pattern. Projects were delivered on time, but clients often felt frustrated by poor communication and a lack of responsiveness. The technical expertise was there, but the relationship and communication side of the business was holding them back.

Instead of outsourcing the problem to external consultants, the firm doubled down on internal development. They launched monthly learning labs, where staff practiced soft skills alongside technical updates. They provided paid time for employees to pursue certifications, pairing senior engineers with younger staff to encourage mentorship. They even invited clients to give feedback in real time, turning those lessons into practical case studies for the team.

Within a year, the change was visible. Project satisfaction scores climbed, repeat business increased, and employee morale rose as staff felt more confident handling client relationships. The investment was not flashy. It did not come with a big marketing push. But like batting practice, it was steady, consistent, and purposeful. Over time, that daily discipline turned into measurable performance gains that elevated both the firm's reputation and its bottom line.

Business Tip

To build a batting practice culture of repetition and skill refinement that strengthens your team:

- Encourage team members to share what they are reading, learning, or experimenting
- Provide structured opportunities for development through workshops, mentorship, or certifications
- Celebrating learning wins, or the practice, not just performance wins
- Create genuine spaces to ask questions, admit gaps, and grow together
- Model the behavior by continuing your own professional education

Learning is not a short stage at the beginning of your career. It is a never-ending routine.

Final Thought

Ken Griffey Jr. played the game with confidence that never faded. Behind that crisp swing was a daily discipline, hours in the batting cage, round after round, long before the crowds entered the stadium. Griffey never stopped learning, never stopped refining, because he knew the game would always present a new challenge and a new pitcher to master.

Great leaders carry that same mindset. The moment you stop learning is the moment you stop leading. Growth cannot be treated as an occasional tune-up. This philosophy must be woven into the DNA of a team. If you want people who thrive under pressure, who trust each other in critical moments, and who improve year after year, you must keep the batting cage open. Make practice more than preparation. Make it a culture of curiosity, a routine of resilience, and a promise that no one is ever finished getting better.

The leaders who endure, like the players who become legends, are the ones who never stop swinging. They treat every lesson, every repetition, every setback, and every success as part of the process. That is how you stay ready for the next pitch and how you build a legacy that lasts long after the season ends.

8

Win at Home – Employee Advocacy Starts Internally

You Cannot Win Championships Until You Win Over Your Home Crowd

Baseball Principle

Before any team boards a bus or plane to face a hostile crowd, they must win at home with each other. The entire organization from the minor league complex league up to the show, needs to embrace a winning culture. Teams at all levels succeed because they know top leadership has their back. The chemistry of a baseball team is not built on gamedays. It is built in the dugout, the locker room, and the bullpen with the tone set by leadership from off-season workouts to the start of Spring Training throughout all levels of the organization.

Championship teams trust each other. They celebrate together, but also challenge each other, and hold each other accountable. When a team hits the road, it does not matter how imposing the opposing fans are if the players are united behind one another.

Championship teams are built on trust cultivated when no one's watching. They celebrate together, hold each other accountable, and move as one. When the Texas Rangers finally broke through in the 2023 season and captured their first World Series title in franchise history, it wasn't about statistics or star power, it was the result of a clubhouse bonded in belief. Ownership invested in this team to win, lifting the team's spirit with dedicated effort and quiet leadership. That unwavering belief in one another turned pressure into purpose and made it possible for them to walk off as champions under their manager Bruce Bochy.

Business Strategy

Companies often focus their energy on external branding, client presentations, and public perception. No message will land with the outside world if it has not already resonated with your own team. Your first ambassadors are not your customers. They are your employees, but their motivation is rooted in the foundation set by management.

If your team is unclear, disconnected, or uninspired, it shows. Culture leaks. Messaging cracks. Productivity stalls. When employees are aligned with the mission, valued in their roles, and confident in the direction, they naturally become advocates. They speak with pride. They share wins. They extend your reputation by word of mouth long before marketing does. Employee advocacy is not a campaign. It is the result of internal trust.

Real-World Example

An accounting firm preparing for a major rebrand initially poured its energy into external marketing, new ads, refreshed materials, and a flurry of client-facing updates. Revenue gains stayed flat, and leadership realized the organizational foundation was not ready.

The firm hit pause on their public push and turned inward. They hosted open forums with partners and associates. They streamlined internal communication, so everyone knew the vision and the why behind it. They provided training so every employee, from senior accountants to support staff, could confidently explain the firm's direction.

Within six months, the tone changed. Employees began sharing the firm's updates with pride. Clients heard the same clear, confident message no matter whom they spoke within the organization. Community referrals grew because people trusted what they were hearing. The rebranding effort's success wasn't driven by the new logo. It happened because the people inside the firm believed in the mission first by focusing internally before executing their external message.

Business Tip

To build internal advocacy and win over your team:

- Share strategic decisions early and transparently so employees understand why
- Recognize staff not just for outcomes, but for embodying company values
- Provide tools and talking points so employees can share the mission accurately and confidently
- Invite feedback from the field to shape messaging and strategy
- Celebrate internal milestones before publicizing external wins

When your team believes in the message, they deliver it better than any ad campaign ever could.

Final Thought

A baseball team cannot quiet a hostile crowd if it is already divided in its own dugout. The same truth applies to business. You cannot win in the marketplace if you are losing unity inside your own walls. Your employees are your home team, and culture is your clubhouse. Before you look outward, look inward. Before you promote a brand, strengthen the bond. Before you chase applause, earn alignment.

The most successful organizations are not built on slogans or campaigns. They are built on shared trust, consistent communication, and a deep sense of belonging. The greatest wins don't start with a public proclamation. They start in private. In conversations where honesty replaces confusion and commitment replaces complacency.

When your team believes in one another, your message carries farther, your brand stands taller, and your victories last longer. Championships are not won in the spotlight. Victories are won in the clubhouse, where unity becomes momentum. Win together inside, and the scoreboard will take care of itself.

9

Rotate the Lineup – Cross-Training & Succession Planning

Championship Teams Prepare with Every Player on the Roster

Baseball Principle

No ball club wins with only nine dependable starters. They win with their entire team's depth. They win with versatility. The teams that last into October are the ones that can rotate the lineup without losing momentum to adapt in any situation.

Whether it is a late-inning pinch hitter, a backup catcher stepping into a clutch role, or a utility infielder covering multiple positions. Successful teams train their bench to be just as ready as their starters. They cross-train. They anticipate. They do not wait for injury or fatigue to prepare the next man up.

Championship rosters are not built on talent alone. They are built on trusting in adaptability. Trust that anyone, on any given day, can deliver when the team needs it most.

Business Strategy

Organizations often operate with a small circle of over-relied-upon high performers. While that may work in the short term, it leaves the team vulnerable to burnout, turnover, and knowledge gaps. Leadership is not just about leading today. It is about preparing others to lead tomorrow.

Succession planning and cross-training are not just human resources initiatives. They are core leadership strategies. They ensure continuity, build resilience, and show employees that the company is invested in their growth, not just their output. Rotating the lineup is not about removing people. It is about elevating more of them to achieve better results.

Real-World Example

A clothing manufacturer faced a challenge when its lead designer unexpectedly took parental leave for their child's adoption. Instead of scrambling, the team simply shifted responsibilities. A junior designer, who had been shadowing projects and learning across accounts, stepped in and carried the workload with confidence.

This did not happen by accident. The firm had built a culture of rotation, assigning stretch roles during downtime, and encouraging employees to understand different aspects of the business. When the moment came, the bench was ready. The company did not miss a beat.

Business Tip

To build a lineup that is flexible and future-ready:

- Identify high-potential employees early and provide them with meaningful shadowing opportunities

- Rotate responsibilities across departments to foster empathy and shared knowledge
- Document key processes so critical tasks do not live with only one person
- Create clear, personalized development plans with roles employees can grow
- Celebrating adaptability just as much as specialization

The teams that last, are the ones that plan for more than today's box score.

Final Thought

Baseball is a game of moments, and sometimes the biggest swing of the season comes from the least expected player. The rookie pinch hitter, the veteran past their prime, or the player fighting through an injury, each with the potential of stepping up when the game is on the line. Those moments are only possible because someone believed in them, trained them, and trusted them before their moment in the spotlight ever found them.

Business is no different. Do not wait for a crisis, a resignation, or an unexpected opportunity to discover who is ready. Build your depth now. Rotate your lineup so experience is shared. Train your bench so they know the playbook. Give your future leaders the chance to grow before they are needed. A winning culture is not defined by a handful of stars. Your culture is defined by what happens when everyone gets a chance to swing, and the whole team knows they can deliver when the count is full, and the game is on the line.

10

Call for the Closer – Knowing When to Let Experts Finish the Job

Success Is Not Just Starting, It Is Finishing

Baseball Principle

Complete game shutouts are a rarity in today's game. In the late innings, fatigue sets in, bat speed catches up, and the margin for error shrinks. That is when the call to the bullpen matters most, not because the starter failed, but because it is time for a specialist. Hall of Famer closers like Mariano Rivera, Goose Gossage, and Lee Smith built their careers on thriving in those moments, entering with the tying run on base, the crowd on its feet, and the game, and sometime the season, hanging in the balance.

Closers are built differently. They feed off pressure, channel the noise, and focus on execution. They are the ones you trust to slam the door shut when there is no tomorrow. The closer's moment is about delivering in the most pivotal spot of the game. However, relief pitchers are not the only ones on the field that can perform in the clutch.

In Game 1 of the 1988 World Series, the Los Angeles Dodgers were down to their final out. Kirk Gibson, hobbled by leg injuries, could barely walk, let alone run. The Dodgers manager Tommy Lasorda called on him anyway, his version of a closer stepping up to the plate. Gibson limped into the batter's box against a future Hall of Famer and one of the most feared relievers in baseball, Dennis Eckersley. With a single perfect swing, Gibson launched a walk-off home run that changed the series. That moment was proof that the closer's job, whether on the mound or at the plate, is about one thing, finishing.

Business Strategy

The instinct to do it all can be hard to shake even for the most accomplished leaders. Company founders and organizational leaders, they often start strong, carry the vision, and stay involved at every stage. High-impact work demands expertise at every level. There comes a time when the best move is to step back and call in the specialist or a closer.

Maybe it is a crisis communications expert during a public relations issue. Maybe it is a specialized legal consultant on a sensitive contract. Maybe it is an art director who can bring a brand story to life in ways others cannot. Whatever the scenario, knowing when to step aside is not giving up authority. It is elevating performance. Leadership is not about being the hero. It is about knowing who can close the game.

Real-World Example

A theme park was struggling to finalize a passholder campaign that had stalled after months of internal work. Deadlines loomed, and tensions rose. Rather than keep grinding, the communications lead brought in an outside consulting firm with deep expertise in campaigns involving behavior change strategies as well as creative media production.

Within three months, the campaign was launched and metrics tracked. The stakeholders were impressed. The internal team still owned the vision, but the closer delivered the win. That shift in mindset turned a struggling project into a model for future collaboration. The theme park knew when they had to call reinforcements to bring in the closer.

Business Tip

To lead like a winning manager who knows when to call for the closer:

- Recognize when your contribution has reached its limit
- Build a trusted bench of specialists before the crisis hits
- Normalize expert collaboration as a strength, not as a crutch
- Share the credit generously when others deliver the final victory
- Focus on team outcomes, not personal ones

The best leaders do not confuse effort with ownership. They focus on getting results.

Final Thought

Baseball teaches us that winning is not always about carrying the game from the first pitch to the last out on your own. Even the greatest starters' arms get tired, hitters adjust, and the margin for error grows razor-thin in the late innings. The real skill is knowing when to step back, when the best way to protect the win is to trust someone else to close out the game.

The same truth applies in any business organization. Leaders who try to do it alone often burn out, drop the ball, or watch hard-earned leads slip away. The most effective leaders have the humility to recognize their limits, the courage to make the handoff, and the wisdom to give the final shot to the person most prepared for it.

Know your limits. Trust your closers. Protect the wins you have worked so hard to achieve. Because in both baseball and business, the teams that finish strong are the ones who understand that passing the ball at the right time, to the right person, is not a sign of weakness, it is the ultimate act of leadership.

🎬 Movie Break: *Field of Dreams* 🎬

Building a Vision Before Others Believe

Baseball Principle

It started as a whisper, carried by the wind through an Iowa cornfield. "If you build it, he will come." This line is more than just a haunting phrase. It becomes a test of belief, a personal mission, and a universal metaphor for every leader who has ever followed an invisible path.

Field of Dreams is not about box scores or home run records. It is about faith in a vision, even when no one else can see it. Ray Kinsella, played with quiet intensity by Kevin Costner, hears a voice and follows it. With no road map, no budget, and no certainty, he risks his family's future to build a baseball field in the middle of a cornfield on his farm.

To outsiders, he is foolish. To his family, he is slipping into delusion. But Ray keeps moving forward. Not because he knows how it will end, but because he somehow knows he must.

This is the purest form of inspirational leadership. You do not wait for applause. You do not chase consensus. You act on conviction. You build because it matters. In that construction, you bring your vision to life.

Business Strategy

The modern business world is obsessed with data, certainty, and validation. Decisions are expected to be grounded in logic, projections, and competitive analysis. Yet, the most groundbreaking ideas often begin in silence.

They begin when someone hears something others do not. A gap in the market. A problem that needs solving. A message that needs saying.

Ray's decision to build a baseball field is not logical, but it is purposeful. He does not know why he is being called to do this, only that it matters. That is how real change begins. Whether it is a bold startup idea, a new public relations campaign, or a marketing strategy that goes against the norm, the greatest innovations are built before others believe in them.

Terence Mann, played by James Earl Jones, becomes a companion in Ray's journey. He challenges Ray. He questions everything. Ultimately, he follows, because he too is seeking something bigger. This mirrors the business world, where many great ideas start in solitude but are shaped and brought to life through trusted partnerships.

The takeaway is clear. The most effective leaders are not just planners. They are builders. They move forward without all the answers. They make bold decisions not because the odds are certain, but because the mission is right. You will not always get agreement. You will not always have support, but you can always choose action.

Real-World Example

Think of entrepreneurs who built billion-dollar companies out of garages and coffee shops. There are many notable nonprofit founders who launched movements with little more than passion and a folding table. Consider the corporate changemakers who challenged internal culture by suggesting ideas that seemed radical at first.

Every one of them heard a whisper. They built something not because the market demanded it, but because their purpose required it. Slowly, and steadily, people came.

One well-known example is Sara Blakely, the founder of Spanx. She started with a vision, no funding, and plenty of skeptics. She believed. She prototyped, persisted, and pitched her way into department stores. Eventually, the world caught up with her vision and just like Ray in the cornfield, she acted before anyone else saw what she saw.

Business Tip

When working toward something others do not yet understand, ask yourself:

- What is my deeper purpose in this project, beyond success or metrics
- What am I building that will outlast short-term wins
- Who are the Terence Mann figures I can invite to challenge and refine my thinking
- Am I willing to act before I am validated
- Do I trust my vision enough to risk comfort in the service of meaning

Progress is rarely made by those who wait for a full plan. It comes from those who move anyway.

Final Thought

Field of Dreams may be about baseball on the surface, but at its heart, it is about faith. Faith in something you cannot yet see, touch, or measure. Ray Kinsella reminds us that vision is not simply imagining the future, it is committing yourself before there is proof, applause, or even understanding from those around you.

In business and in life, there will be moments when you hear that quiet voice urging you forward. It may be a whisper of an idea, a calling others cannot comprehend, or a dream so fragile it feels risky to speak aloud. Vision is built in those moments. It is hammered into place with every decision to keep going when logic says stop.

You will build long before anyone shows up. You will plant seeds without knowing if the harvest will come. If you stay true to the mission, if you build the field with purpose and conviction, people will come. Not always right away, and not always in the way you expect, but they will come because they recognize something rare. People see value in someone who built not for applause, but for the cause. That is the kind of vision that outlasts trends, that inspires generations, and that turns a dream into a legacy. That is the field worth building. That is a dream worth chasing. That is why people will most definitely come.

⚾ Section 2: Collaboration ⚾

11

Play Small Ball When Needed – Tactical vs. Strategic Thinking

Knowing When a Small Act Delivers the Biggest Victory

Baseball Principle

The strategy of playing smallball may not light up the scoreboard with towering home runs, but it does light up the win column when executed correctly. For decades, managers like Whitey Herzog with the St. Louis Cardinals in the 1980s, and Ned Yost with the 2015 World Series Champion Kansas City Royals, thrived on this approach by leaning into bunts, steals, and hit-and-runs instead of pure slugging and raw power. The philosophy demanded discipline, precision, and a willingness to put the team's success over individual statistics.

As analytics ushered in an era of launch angles and exit velocity, smallball tactics have faded to a degree from the current MLB spotlight. But not everywhere. The Cleveland Guardians have embraced their own version, dubbed "Guards-Ball." This strategy is built on contact hitting, aggressive baserunning, and situational awareness. In 2022 under manager Terry Francona, Cleveland was dead last in the league in home runs but finished first in the American League Central. This championship happened because they moved runners, avoided strikeouts, and stayed relentlessly focused on the next 90 feet in front of them.

Managers who succeed with smallball are masters of the moment. They know when to bunt, when to run, and when to trust the next guy up. It is not about playing it safe, as it is about playing it smart. Being strategic is the key to fitting your team's best resources at the right time through a holistic team first approach.

Business Strategy

Strategy provides the teams with the vision, a true North Star. However, results lie in execution, the right moves at the right time, is what turns vision into reality. In the corporate world, leaders often gravitate toward big plays with five-year plans, transformational initiatives, and high stakes product launches. No one will ever complain about hitting a home run. However, every member of your team may not be able to hit one out of the yard. Focusing only on the long ball can lead to missed opportunities by aligning your team to their individual strengths.

A leader who practices smallball in business knows how to read the entire field. They listen to frontline employees, scan for quick wins, and understand that timely action. Even modest victories build credibility and trust. They know that calling a customer personally, tweaking a system based on user feedback, or recognizing a team member's effort today creates the culture and momentum needed for tomorrow's breakthroughs.

Smart leaders do not choose between strength and strategic tactics. They master the art of knowing when to swing for the fences and when to bunt the run home. The best leaders know playing small ball is sometimes a more efficient way to victory than brute strength.

Real-World Example

In the heart of a major urban corridor, a rail line was preparing for a major overhaul. Plans were made for new branding, a mobile app launch, and a multi-year rider experience plan. Strategy meetings filled calendars. Consultants and engineers were engaged. The vision was big, bold, and expensive while the public impatiently wanted answers.

As all eyes looked to the future, daily riders were growing frustrated with poor signage, unclear schedules, and communication breakdowns. The agency was losing ground in the present. They did not focus on the little things that had the most impact on their customers on a daily and routine basis.

One staff member, a bilingual communications coordinator, took initiative. They spearheaded a series of micro-efforts including pop-up rider feedback booths, real-time schedule flyers in multiple languages, and short social videos introducing drivers by name. These small acts re-humanized the agency. Riders felt seen. Compliments funneled in. Ridership shifted upward within weeks. When the big strategic changes finally rolled out, the community was already leaning in with renewed trust. It was not strategy versus tactics. It was strategy supported by tactical wins by doing the little things right.

Business Tip

Tactical execution builds the bridge to strategic success. To apply small ball thinking:

- Identify three high-impact, low-cost actions you or your team can take this week
- Seek what can be done today to earn trust, move forward, or fix friction
- Make space for team members to propose and own ideas
- Remember, progress is cumulative as getting on base adds up to runs

Map your quarterly strategies, but stack your weekly tasks with achievable, tactical wins. The small ball moves throughout your organization keeps putting runs on the scoreboard.

Final Thought

Some of baseball's most unforgettable victories are built on moments that never make the highlight reel, the perfectly placed squeeze bunt, the daring steal with two outs, the sacrifice fly that trades personal glory for the game-winning run. These plays may not dazzle the crowd, but they deliver where it counts with the final score.

In work life, the same truth applies. Bold visions can inspire, but it is the relentless attention to detail, the willingness to make the unselfish move, and the discipline to execute the fundamentals that truly shape outcomes. You will not always need the towering home run. Sometimes, the smartest move is the one that quietly advances the runner, sets up the next opportunity, and keeps the momentum alive.

Play small ball when the moment calls for it. In doing so, you prove that leadership is not about chasing attention, it is about making the right play at the right time. Leaders need their teams to care enough to play smart on every pitch, knowing that championships are sometimes won with one small deliberate and well-executed decision at a time.

12

Swing for the Fences, When It Counts – Calculated Big Bets

Making Bold, Calculated Moves When the Moment Demands It

Baseball Principle

Small ball is absolutely an effective strategy. However, there is a distinct electricity in the ballpark when the stakes are high, and the game is on the line where something big needs to happen. Think of Bill Mazeroski's walk-off home run in Game 7 of the 1960 World Series that lifted the Pittsburgh Pirates to a stunning 10-9 victory over the New York Yankees, which was the only Game 7 in World Series history to end with a walk-off home run. Remember Reggie Jackson's legendary three-home-run performance in Game 6 of the 1977 World Series, earning him the nickname "Mr. October." These were not reckless hacks but big swings at the right moment which are strategic tactics too. These were huge hacks taken by players who were prepared, focused, and fearless in the moment.

Swinging for the fences is not about showboating. It is about understanding the game situation, trusting your preparation, and committing when the time is right. Power hitters know not to waste energy chasing a pitch out of their sweet spot. They study opposing pitchers, wait for the mistake, and then unload.

Managers, too, have their big moments. When a team is behind late and a flamethrowing pitcher faces a cleanup slugger, sometimes the call is simply to let him swing. The same strategy applies to life. Managers know when something bigger is needed and the moment is right, because some at-bats can change everything with one swing.

Business Strategy

Game-changing moments do not come every day. When they do, they often arrive quietly, an email from a potential business partner, a market shift you anticipated, a proposal opportunity you are uniquely suited to win. These are the moments that separate incremental progress from exponential growth.

Taking a big swing does not mean gambling. It means you have studied analytics, you know the scouting report, and the situation puts your team in a position to deliver. A calculated big bet is built on research, readiness, and confidence. Leaders must place their trust in their people, their plan, and their purpose.

It might be launching a new company-wide initiative, entering an emerging market, or proposing a transformational contract. Leaders who thrive in these moments do not shy away from the magnitude. They clarify the risk, rally their teams, and swing with conviction.

Real-World Example

An educational consulting firm had spent years building a solid reputation for private school work. Their sweet spot was school safety campaigns, outreach, and project communications which resulted in steady, dependable projects that kept them in the game.

Then came the opportunity of a lifetime with a statewide educational campaign contract that would triple their typical scope and put them on a national radar. The safer move would have been to pass, or partner as a subcontractor. The firm's founder saw it differently. This was their swing when the game was on the line.

They assembled an elite proposal team, including creatives, strategists, and data analysts. They brought in a media partner with national reach and built a proposal that told not just a story, but a vision. Their proposal was compelling, deeply aligned with the client's mission, and backed by both metrics and passion.

They won. Not just the contract, but a new confidence, visibility, and influence across their industry. The swing was bold, but not blind. It was the culmination of years of groundwork, relationships, and readiness.

Business Tip

When you feel the moment calling for a big swing:

- Clarify the stakes by knowing what is at risk and the potential reward.
- Align the opportunity that connects to your purpose, strengths, and values.
- Assess your readiness with your infrastructure, talent, and resources to succeed or to absorb a swing and miss
- Rally your team because big swings require full buy-in by communicating clearly and decisively.
- Trust your preparation because if you have done the work, do not flinch.

A big swing should not surprise you with undo pressure. It should feel like the moment you have been preparing for all along.

Final Thought

Some at-bats change more than games, but careers. Some decisions redefine companies. There will come a moment when your leadership is measured not by how steady you have been, but by how boldly you respond when opportunity finally arrives. Swinging for the fences is not about showmanship, it is about readiness. The quiet preparation that allows you to recognize your pitch the instant it crosses the plate.

Great leaders know the difference between swinging wildly and swinging wisely. They understand that the fear of missing on a swing can never outweigh the chance to make history. Whether the result is a towering home run or a deep fly that moves the winning run into scoring position, what matters is that you saw the moment for what it was, and acted without hesitation.

The scoreboard will not record your doubts. It will record your impact and the results. When that perfect pitch comes, middle-in, belt-high in your wheelhouse, do not freeze. Step in. Lock eyes on the target. Breathe deep. Swing like the future of the game is in your hands. You are prepared. You are ready because this is your moment.

13

Watch the Scoreboard – Data-Driven Decision-Making

Let Metrics Guide Your Strategy, Not Just Validate It

Baseball Principle

The scoreboard in baseball is not just a tally of runs, hits, and errors. It is a living dashboard of the game's context. It tells the story behind every pitch in the narrative of outs, inning, pitch count, base runners, who is on deck, and which part of the lineup is due up. Great managers and players glance at it not out of habit, but because it helps them make the next decision.

Hall of Famer Tony La Russa was one of the game's most cerebral managers. He was known for reading the scoreboard like a chess board. He knew when to pull a starter early, shift the defense, or send in a pinch hitter, not because he had a hunch, but because the scoreboard told him the odds, the timing, and the need. When the Moneyball analytics transformed the game, teams like the Oakland A's, under their general manager Billy Beane, proved that reading the numbers could close the gap between budget and success.

Baseball is not played with your gut alone. The scoreboard is the truth teller. It shows what is happening, not what you hope is happening. The best in the game use it to respond, recalibrate, and outthink the opposition in real time with the data at your disposal.

Business Strategy

Every leader has a scoreboard no matter the industry they compete within. It is not just revenue and profit but also employee turnover, social media sentiment, project completion rates, and customer feedback. Too many organizations either ignore the numbers, massage them for optics, or weaponize them to prove a point rather than to learn.

Real leadership means embracing what the data reveals, even when it is uncomfortable. It means having the humility to change course along with the discipline to stay with what is working. When you let data lead, not just follow, you transform guesswork into informed action.

Just like in baseball, you cannot manage if you do not know the score. You cannot win the game if you are playing blind without the data you need.

Real-World Example

An e-commerce company had been celebrating a record quarter of online traffic. The chief marketing officer pushed out press releases, internal emails, and social posts touting the growth. One analytics intern noticed something odd. Despite the spike in visitors, conversion rates had quietly dropped 20 percent.

Rather than dismiss it, the leadership team dove in. Analytics tools revealed a glitch on the mobile checkout page, where load times on tablets had doubled. Instead of celebrating vanity metrics, the team pivoted to user experience. They fixed the technical issue, relaunched the site, and monitored bounce rates daily. The next quarter, conversions returned stronger than ever.

The intern's observation, and the team's willingness to follow the scoreboard instead of the story, turned a miss into a win. It doesn't matter who on the team contributes as every member of the team can see the scoreboard.

Business Tip

To become a data-driven leader:

- Define success early and know what metrics matter before launching any initiative
- Check in often and do not wait until the end to measure impact, track in progress
- Balance perspectives by combining leading indicators (what is likely to happen) with lagging indicators (what already happened)
- Empower visibility with building dashboards your entire team can access and understand
- Stay curious and use data to surface new questions, not just confirm old assumptions

Let your data be your compass, not your rearview mirror.

Final Thought

The scoreboard never lies. It demands the courage to truly look at it honestly. It does not measure your intentions, your passion, or how hard you worked. It measures what happened. It will not flatter you or soften the truth, but if you have the humility to face it without excuse, it becomes one of your most powerful tools.

Leadership is not simply about holding a vision but about making the right adjustments when the scoreboard tells you the game has changed. It means pulling the pitcher not because it feels comfortable, but because the data says it is time. Sometimes it is a bold substitution. Sometimes it is the cautious hold. Either way, the call must match the reality in front of you, not the one you wish were true.

Whether you are mounting a comeback in the late innings or protecting a fragile lead, the scoreboard is your compass. Read it closely. Trust it fully. Let it sharpen your focus so you can win not by hope, but by informed, intentional action. In the end, the scoreboard does more than keep the count. It keeps you honest, it keeps you accountable, and when you respect it, it helps you finish on top.

14

The Infield Shift – Strategic Flexibility & Change Management

Adapt to the Situation Without Losing Your Structure

Baseball Principle

Defensive shifts were once considered radical. For a brief time, shifts were a hallmark of modern baseball strategy until they were outlawed by Major League Baseball in 2023. Prior to the rule change, when a left-handed slugger like Joey Gallo or David Ortiz stepped to the plate, the infield no longer stayed in their traditional spots. The shortstop might slide over to shallow right, the third baseman might take second, and the second baseman might become a roving outfielder. To the untrained eye, it looked chaotic, but it was calculated.

We can still learn from this concept as infield shifts are the product of data, discipline, and decisiveness. Coaches analyze batter's spray charts, tendencies, and probabilities to place defenders where the ball is most likely to go. It is not a gamble as it is a response rooted in data. While the shift does not always work, it gives the defense its best shot at success in the moment.

When Tampa Bay Rays manager Kevin Cash led his underdog roster to compete in the World Series in 2020, shifting was central to his approach. The Rays could not outspend other teams with their payroll, but they could out-think them with strategic and tactical ploys. They adjusted constantly, not just because they had to, but because they were built that way. Great teams always must be ready and play to their own unique advantage.

Business Strategy

Many leaders stick with what has worked in the past until it no longer does. The comfort of tradition, familiar organizational charts, or entrenched routines can become a trap. The most resilient organizations understand that the conditions around them are always shifting. The question is, will you be adaptable to the shift.

Strategic flexibility means staying anchored in your purpose, but elastic in your playbook. It means listening to real-time feedback, watching the metrics, and adjusting your team's alignment without losing its cohesion. It is not about being immediately reactive. It is about being responsive.

Think of a product manager shifting resources from a feature that users are ignoring to one that is gaining traction. Or a CEO reallocating staff to a growing region instead of sticking to historical territories. These are modern infield shifts that are executed with clarity, not panic. Being static is the greater risk as strategic movement is what keeps you in the game.

Real-World Example

A family-owned specialty grocer had long thrived on in-store experience, samples, cooking demos, and community events. When the pandemic hit, their foot traffic plummeted. Competitors with slick e-commerce platforms started winning their long-term customers.

Rather than cling to tradition, the leadership team acted fast. They partnered with local tech startups to launch a digital storefront within two weeks. Staff who once ran in-store events became virtual content creators with a viral reach. Parking lots became curbside pickup hubs. Weekly newsletters pivoted to recipe bundles and meal kits. It was a total infield shift.

Not only did they survive the disruption, but they also built a new hybrid model that outperformed their pre-pandemic numbers. They kept their identity intact the entire time.

Business Tip

To embed flexibility into your organization's culture:

- Assign someone to track shifts in technology, customer behavior, and regulations
- Design contingency options and rehearse responses before a crisis forces one
- Cross-functional teams can adjust faster than isolated departments
- Highlight team members who suggest improvements, not just execute tasks
- Clarify what is fixed and what is flexible as purpose should be firm, processes should not

Shifting your infield is not about abandoning your game plan. It is about increasing your chances to win with the tools and information you have today.

Final Thought

When certain batters came to the plate, the players on the field knew to glance at the dugout for the manager to signal the shift. It is quiet, yet decisive. Not a sign of panic, but of poise. It tells everyone, we see the challenge, and we are ready to meet it.

Shift moments come without warning in a business setting. Market swings, a competitor emerges, a disruption hits can occur even with the best laid plans. The scoreboard will not wait. However, when your team is trained to move, when your culture is built to adapt, change becomes second nature.

Adaptation is not a sidestep from leadership. It is leadership itself. Great leaders prepare teams that not only execute the plan. They adjust the plan without hesitation. When the hitter at the plate pulls everything to right, do not stay rooted out of habit or pride. Shift the infield. Trust your preparation and move to where the opportunity lives now.

The teams that move together, win together and the leaders who guide them are remembered not for standing still, but for making the right move at the right time. Sometimes winning means moving from where you have always been to where the opportunity is now.

15

Get the Win, Not the Spotlight – Innovation Without Vanity Metrics

Make Bold Moves That Deliver Real Value, Not Just Headlines

Baseball Principle

Steven Kwan is not the most intimidating player on the field. He does not chase tape-measure home runs or viral highlights. Instead, he wins games with the subtleties that most fans barely notice. Stretching a single into a double, dropping down a perfect bunt, making a split-second read on a fly ball, or by impressively making contact in over ninety percent of swings he takes. A two-time All-Star and four-time Gold Glove winner in left field for the Cleveland Guardians, Kwan is redefining value in today's power-obsessed game.

Like the great leadoff hitters before him, Kwan changes the game without demanding the spotlight by doing the little things with big impact. His hustle and accurate arm pressures the defense. His awareness creates opportunities. His fundamentals keep his team in control. None of it may trend on social media, but in the dugout, everyone knows those plays change everything.

Business Strategy

There is a dangerous temptation to equate visibility with value. Leaders sometimes chase arrogant metrics, impressions, headlines, follower counts, believing that attention equals impact. The true Steven Kwan contributors in an organization prove otherwise. They deliver consistent results, strengthen the team's foundation, and make smart, timely moves that set the table for the big wins.

Real innovation often starts quietly. It might be an internal process that eliminates bottlenecks, a small design tweak that improves customer experience, or a subtle shift in strategy that positions the company for long-term growth. These moments may never be publicized, but they make all the difference.

Real-World Example

At a fast-growing autonomous vehicle startup, onboarding customer numbers were dragging. The instinct was to launch a flashy marketing campaign to drive more signups. Instead, a junior developer looked inward. They discovered the real problem, an inefficient identification customer verification flow, and redesigned it to be faster, clearer, and more user-friendly. The fix reduced drop-offs by 42 percent and increased completed signups.

No press release. No conference stage with flashing lights. Just results that made the whole company stronger. Like Kwan taking the extra base, the move might not have been glamorous, but it advanced the game in a way that mattered.

Business Tip

To lead and innovate without chasing the spotlight:

- Define success through measurable outcomes, not public praise
- Master your fundamentals before chasing the next big move
- Empower problem-solvers who focus on substance over style
- Reward progress that strengthens the team, even if it is unseen
- Let the scoreboard, not the headlines, prove your value

Final Thought

Steven Kwan reminds us that greatness is not always flashy or imposing. Both in baseball and in business, the play that shifts the game often goes unnoticed by the crowd but is celebrated in the clubhouse and back at the office. True leadership is not about who gets the credit, it is about moving your team forward, sometimes in ways only they will fully appreciate internally.

Strategic consistency builds trust. Smart timing creates opportunity. The willingness to act, especially when no one is watching, is what turns good teams into champions. Stealing second base may not look like much from the stands, but it changes everything for the team that needs that runner in scoring position.

As a leader, you do not need to go viral to make an impact. You need to see the gap, trust your preparation, and take the step that matters. Quiet moves, made with intention, can echo far beyond their moment.

The next time you have a chance to improve something, even if no one is watching, make the move. Make the hustle play and let your results do the talking. Every brick is a building block for team victory.

16

Know When to Take a Walk – Negotiation & Tactical Retreats

Strategic Restraint Is Sometimes the Most Powerful Move You Can Make

Baseball Principle

Not every at-bat ends with a swing, and that is by design. Some of the greatest hitters in baseball history, including Barry Bonds and Hank Aaron, earned reputations not just for home run power but for discipline. They knew the strike zone better than the umpire, and they refused to chase pitches outside it.

Barry Bonds walked 2,558 times in his career, the most in MLB history. In 2004 alone, he was intentionally walked 120 times, an astonishing signal of both respect and fear. Many of his walks came from patience, not power. Bonds could sit back, let borderline pitches pass, and take his base with a quiet nod. No bat flip. No highlight reel. Just strategy.

Taking a walk is not about giving up, it is about gaining ground. It puts pressure on the pitcher. It creates opportunities for your team, and it shows that sometimes, the most powerful move is restraint. Baseball teaches this truth, swinging at everything does not make you a hero. It makes you easy to beat.

Business Strategy

There is often unspoken pressure in business to always be in motion, to seize every opportunity, say yes to every deal, and swing at every pitch that comes your way. Maturity is marked by the ability to pause. The power to say no. The wisdom to walk away.

A smart leader knows that not every contract is worth signing, not every partnership is worth the tradeoffs, and not every moment is worth pressing forward. Sometimes the win comes from restraint by recognizing when the timing is off, the terms are wrong, or the cost is too high.

Strategic retreat is not surrender. It is strength. Walking away is not a failure. It is often the prelude to your best decision.

Real-World Example

A branding and advertising agency had just landed on a shortlist for a massive national campaign that promised visibility, revenue, and prestige. As the negotiation unfolded, the client demanded full content ownership, access to internal audience data, and a year-long exclusivity clause that would prevent the agency from working with other clients in their growing niche.

The opportunity looked glamorous. However, the CEO took a breath. They met with their leadership team. They reviewed the deal through the lens of long-term growth and not just this month's win. Together, they made the collective decision and walked away.

It stung for a moment but just three months later, a tech client with aligned values approached them for a collaborative, non-exclusive engagement. That campaign became their most successful yet by launching them into new markets without compromising their autonomy. By taking the walk, they protected their mission and made room for something better.

Business Tip

To build strength through strategic restraint:

- Before any deal, define what you will not compromise
- Consider not just the short-term win, but the long-term cost
- Create a culture where a "no" is respected because it gives your team the confidence to pause or pivot
- Say yes when it serves your mission, not your ego
- A walk can be a winning move when it sets up future success

Sometimes the smartest way forward is taking one step back.

Final Thought

Leadership is not a contest to see who swings the hardest with the biggest bat. It is a discipline built on timing, clarity, and the courage to act with purpose. Sometimes a walk even scores a run. Joe Maddon famously ordered an intentional walk of the Texas Rangers' Corey Seager with the bases loaded during his tenure as the Los Angeles Angels manager.

The scoreboard will not show restraint, but your team will feel it. They will see a leader who plays the long game, who does not chase bad pitches, and who understands that the count does not define you. The next opportunity is what can give the team the true definition.

When the pressure rises and the pitch sails outside your zone, do not flinch. Do not chase. Take the walk. You may not hear the roar of the crowd, but you will know you made the right call for your team, your values, and your future. By taking the walk, you give your team the chance to deliver the smarter and more profitable swing when it matters most.

17

Cover the Bases – Comprehensive Project Planning

Details Win Games Before They Begin

Baseball Principle

Covering the bases is more than a metaphor, it is a tactical imperative. When a ball is hit, every player has a role. The pitcher does not solely focus on throwing strikes. He is backing up throws to third or home. The catcher is directing traffic. The infield rotates. Outfielders anticipate the play, not just the batted ball. It is a finely choreographed response to chaos.

Think back to the 2011 World Series, Game 6, when the St. Louis Cardinals came from behind, twice, to keep the game alive. In the bottom of the 9th, David Freese tied the game with a two-run triple. He then won it in the 11th with a walk-off home run. While his heroics are the highlight, the Cardinals' survival that night was indeed a team effort with tight defense, heads-up baserunning, and role players like Freese stepping up alongside stars to keep them alive for Game 7. He even declined induction into the Cardinals Hall of Fame because he respected his role in the memorable postseason heroics, while beloved by fans, did not equate to the sustained career contributions he felt the honor represents.

Championship teams do not just react well. They prepare better and know their roles to honor the team. They drill situational plays until they are second nature. Because they know that one missed assignment, a cutoff man out of place, a pitcher failing to back up third, can cost the game. In the game of inches, details do not slow you down. They set you free.

Business Strategy

Covering the bases means investing time upfront to plan smart, define roles, and identify risks before the pitch is thrown. Teams that rush into action without alignment end up fielding problems they could have easily prevented. Missed deadlines. Overlooked approvals. Mismatched expectations. These are the business equivalent of letting a runner score from first on a single on a Little League home run.

Strong planning does not eliminate surprises, but it equips your team to handle them with confidence. When responsibilities are clear, timelines are realistic. When contingencies are mapped, your people stop guessing and start executing. They have room to solve problems creatively, because they are not consumed by chaos.

Great execution is not a matter of chance. It is the result of consistent, intentional preparation, before the spotlight ever turns on.

Real-World Example

A municipal planning department in a fast-growing city received a sudden grant to launch a community outreach initiative with a hard 90-day deadline. The instinct was to start designing the campaign immediately. The department's public affairs leader, an Army veteran turned communications director, hit pause.

Instead, they led a five-day project planning sprint. Roles were assigned, stakeholder maps were created, translators were secured for non-English-speaking communities, and every deliverable was tied to a timeline with risk buffers built in. They even scheduled dry runs for community town halls to troubleshoot before the public saw anything.

The results then showed all materials launched on time. Community feedback was overwhelmingly positive. Media coverage praised the clarity of messaging. The city received follow-up funding due to its professionalism and transparency.

Success was not magic. It was preparation and it covered every base.

Business Tip

To ensure your projects start strong and stay on course:

- Define roles, goals, timelines, and expectations up front
- Help your team see not just what is due, but how it all connects
- Prevent the small stuff from becoming big issues by communicating often
- Build a risk matrix and identify backup options
- Revisit the plan weekly, even daily, and adjust as needed

Great project planning is like strong defense in baseball. When done well, it looks simple, but only because it was designed to manage complexity long before the play ever happened.

Final Thought

It is tempting to chase the headlines or the grand idea whether on the ballfield or in the boardroom. Games are most often won behind the scenes through quiet preparation, deliberate alignment, and teammates who know exactly where to be and when.

Planning is not about control. Planning is about clarity. When your team understands the full layout of the field and intricacies of the ballpark, hesitation disappears. Movements become instinctive. Trust builds. Problems are anticipated, and the routine plays look effortless.

Cover your bases. Every one of them. Do not assume, do not rush, and do not wait until the play is already in motion. Give your team the advantage before the first pitch is thrown.

Greatness is not improvised. It is built with organization, with structure, and with the discipline that allows your team to deliver excellence every time. Covering your bases leaves nothing to chance.

18

Trade Deadline Decisions – Pivoting at the Right Moment

Knowing When to Make the Move That Changes Everything

Baseball Principle

Every year, the late season MLB trade deadline marks a defining fork in the road. Each team's front office must choose, are they buyers, sellers, or builders for the future. That decision drives what comes next. Bold trades can ignite a playoff run. Hesitation can stall a season. It is not just about acquiring talent. The real skill is about knowing what the team needs most, and when.

Consider the Houston Astros in 2017. Just hours before the trade deadline, they traded for Cy Young Award Justin Verlander. That one decision transformed them from a strong team into a World Series winner. The trade shifted energy in the clubhouse, lifted expectations, and set the tone for a title run.

Not every trade is about landing a star. Steve Pearce was considered a role player, a journeyman first baseman and outfielder who had already played for six different MLB teams. When the Toronto Blue Jays dealt him to the Boston Red Sox for a minor league infielder, the trade barely made headlines, but Pearce became a postseason force. In the 2018 World Series against the Los Angeles Dodgers, he hit three home runs, drove in eight runs, and delivered clutch hits. He was named World Series MVP, helping the Red Sox win their fourth title in 15 years.

Sometimes, it is about clearing the bench, giving younger players a shot, or building depth for what comes next. The smartest GMs know when to buy, when to sell, and most importantly when to pivot. Waiting too long is rarely forgiven by the standings.

Business Strategy

Organizations face their own trade deadline moments in times when holding on becomes more dangerous than letting go. It might be a floundering product, a stalled initiative, or a once-promising partnership that no longer fits. These are the moments that test a leader's courage.

Strategic pivots require a sober assessment of what is working and what is not. They demand leaders who can look past sunk costs, self-indulgence, and nostalgia to focus on what will move the mission forward now.

Great leaders are not afraid to say, this is no longer serving us. They are willing to reallocate resources, reassign roles, and reset direction, even when it is uncomfortable. A trade is not a surrender. It is a decision to compete more effectively with what comes next, especially when it is uncomfortable.

Real-World Example

A nonprofit dedicated to youth empowerment had invested heavily in a new mobile app that promised to boost engagement with teens and parents. The launch was promising with strong downloads, media coverage, and excitement from community partners.

But six weeks in, usage had dropped sharply. Feedback revealed a mismatch with teens preferring messaging platforms they already used, and parents finding the app confusing. Rather than doubling down out of pride, the leadership team huddled.

They made a bold call to shut down the app, shift to a mobile-optimized website, and launched an SMS-based mentorship update system using tools teens already trusted. Within three months, their engagement rate more than doubled, and the initiative was praised in a regional innovation showcase. They made the trade, and it changed the game.

Business Tip

When facing a pivot point, use these guidelines:

- Let knowledge and data lead, not sunk cost or personal bias
- Be clear about what no longer aligns with your mission or strategy
- Use scenario planning to weigh risks, timing, and potential upside
- Bring your team and stakeholders along with transparency and purpose
- Especially when roles, relationships, or resources are impacted

A smart pivot protects momentum and positions your team to win the game and the season.

Final Thought

Baseball teaches us that seasons are defined not only by how you start, but by how you adapt when the landscape changes. Trade deadline moves are rarely about just adding talent. They are about reading the moment, knowing what your team truly needs, and having the courage to make the call before the opportunity passes.

Momentum in a business setting is every bit fragile. Opportunities do not wait for you to feel ready. The longer you hesitate, the faster they disappear. Often, it is the silence of indecision, not the sting of a misstep, that costs teams' their chance at something greater.

The pivot is not a sign of uncertainty. It is a mark of leadership. It says you are willing to move toward what will serve your mission, even if it means letting go of what is comfortable. It is about acting while the path is still open, knowing the future will not slow down for you.

Sometimes, the season is saved not by having your players simply try harder, but by making the move that redefines the game. When you are the one who has the vision to see it and the resolve to act. Your team will remember, not just that you made the right call, but that you refused to let the moment pass you by.

19

The Double Steal – Coordinated Campaigns Across Channels

How Synchronization Amplifies Your Message and Impact

Baseball Principle

The double steal is one of baseball's most electrifying plays, driven not by speed alone but by perfect synchronization. When two runners take off at the same time, it creates controlled chaos for the defense. Uncertainty forces hesitation, and that hesitation is the point. When executed with precision, the double steal transforms an ordinary moment into a game-changing opportunity.

Stories of the past share highlights of Jackie Robinson and Pee Wee Reese, who used aggressive base running and daring coordination to force mistakes. The double steal only works when both players trust the timing, understand the signs, and go all in without hesitation. One runner draws the attention. The other takes the prize.

The magic lies not in speed, but in strategy, timing, and trust. When those align, the impossible becomes possible.

Business Strategy

In marketing, a double steal is a well-timed, multi-channel, multi-team effort where every element is orchestrated to work in sync. It is not about doing more. It is about doing it together.

A brand message alone might get overlooked. A post might disappear in a social media feed. A press release might go unread. However, when those elements are synchronized, where public relations, digital, outreach, and internal teams move with shared purpose, the impact multiplies. Each channel reinforces the other. Momentum builds in a true systems management approach.

Unfortunately, most organizations operate in silos. Communications teams work separately from operations and the customer experience teams. Outreach happens without insights from leadership. A department launches a campaign without looping in analytics. The resulting in a fragmented message that feels disconnected and underwhelming with a fragmented organization looking out for their individual goals.

The best teams plan like base stealers, discreetly, boldly, and together. They commit to coordination, not confusion. Operating effectively as a team on all system cylinders.

Real-World Example

A state department of transportation planned a public rollout of a new express toll lane system along a major highway corridor. They knew that press releases and signage would not be enough to overcome confusion or resistance. They went for a double steal approach, but in their specific case, more like a triple steal, with three phases.

Phase one: A 60-second animated explanation video launched simultaneously across YouTube, Facebook, Instagram, and X, walking viewers through how the system worked.

Phase two: The same day, printed inserts arrived in water bills and electric bills targeting local households, including those same infographics in a social media campaign.

Phase three: Outreach teams hosted real-time events at commuter stops and community events, handing out printed guides in multiple languages and answering questions face-to-face while going door to door presenting personal information.

Meanwhile, agency spokespeople were featured in the media on radio and TV, reinforcing the same message. This synchronization created clarity and energy. Enrollment jumped 42 percent within 60 days, customer feedback was overwhelmingly positive, and confusion, historically a barrier for toll programs, was dramatically reduced.

Each effort supported the others. No message stood alone because the system worked with cohesion. Every aspect supported the other to achieve overall success.

Business Tip

To run your version of a double steal:

- Every channel and team should speak from the same core purpose
- Don't cut and paste, but craft messages suited to the audience and medium
- Sequence your efforts so they build momentum, rather than compete for attention
- Share assets, calendars, and talking points in advance without company silos
- Review what worked across all departments, and apply the learnings to future efforts

Synchronization beats saturation. True team communication beats noise and motion.

Final Thought

The double steal is one of the purest expressions of trust and timing on the diamond. It only works when the runners involved believe in the plan. The runners commit to the sign without hesitation. Effective leaders trust their team to read the moment with absolute clarity. The execution is bold, calculated, and unified. One hesitation, one missed signal, and the play collapses. When the strategy meets opportunity and it all clicks, it can tilt the entire game.

Leadership and communication work the same way. The best campaigns and the most effective strategies succeed not because of a single star performer, but because every person moves in rhythm with the others. When departments align, when leaders share why as well as what, and when every contributor knows exactly how their role fits into the larger play, the impact becomes exponential. Messages do not just land, they stick, they spread, and they inspire real action.

Too many organizations lose momentum because they act like isolated baserunners, each with their own read of the game, each moving on their own plans. Real power is in the alignment. Specialness is in movement that is coordinated, confident, and driven by shared purpose. That is how great campaigns catch the competition off guard, move the mission forward, and win by delivering results that stick.

20

Opening Day Matters – Launch Strategies & First Impressions

Why the First Communication Sets the Tone for the Entire Campaign

Baseball Principle

Opening Day is sacred in baseball. It is more than just the first game of the season. It is truly a ceremony based on belief and hope in the future. Across the country, ballparks are filled with optimism. Patriotic bunting adorns the fences around the field signaling something special is happening today. First pitches are thrown by community heroes or legends of the game. The national anthem is often sung by a celebrity. It is a declaration that a new chapter is beginning.

Historically, teams like the New York Yankees or the San Francsico Giants use Opening Day not just to introduce lineups, but to showcase their generational identity. They display legacy, tradition, and focus. Even rebuilding teams understand the power of the first impression. In 2024, the Chicago White Sox, coming off one of the worst seasons in MLB history with 121 losses, still over 31,000 filled the stadium with hope on Opening Day the next season. Every new beginning starts a tone of resilience that can help transform the franchise over the next few months of a long schedule.

Opening Day is not about the final score from the last season. It is about how you show up being focused, prepared, and with hope in the journey ahead. How you begin often determines how long the crowd stays with you through the ups and downs of the season.

Business Strategy

Every new company process or management change has its own Opening Day. Much like at the ballpark, your audience is watching closely. They want to know what you believe in and what you are offering. They want to know if you are ready and respect the attention your audience is giving you.

A careless rollout sends the wrong message. If your materials are inconsistent, your channels out of sync, or your team unprepared, your audience notices and judges you accordingly. A launch that is crisp, confident, and coordinated signals professionalism, purpose, and pride.

The first impression is not about perfection. It is about presence. When you step onto the field, whether that is a stage, a livestream, or a homepage, you tell the world that your team is ready and that you care.

Real-World Example

A local restaurant chain serving a diverse community in a small city had always relied on phone orders, walk-ins, and third-party delivery services. When they launched their own mobile ordering and loyalty app, they knew success would hinge not just on the technology, it would hinge on the rollout strategy.

They treated launch day like it was opening night at a flagship location:

- Local radio stations ran preview segments the night before, thanks to early media outreach highlighting exclusive launch-day specials
- Table tents, takeout bags, and storefront windows featured QR codes so customers could download the app instantly while dining or picking up orders
- Community partners, including neighborhood associations and youth sports leagues, helped spread the concept
- Frontline staff were trained to walk guests through downloading the app and redeeming their first reward
- A bilingual welcome video featuring the owner and a longtime server premiered on launch day, inviting the community to be part of the celebration

The results were more than 10,000 downloads in the first week, a 92 percent satisfaction score in follow-up surveys, and a surge in repeat orders. Customers did not just use the app, they felt like they were part of something new and exciting. It worked because the launch was not treated as a technical update. It was treated like Opening Day.

Business Tip

To make your next launch feel like Opening Day:

- Reverse-engineer your messaging calendar from the go-live date
- Internal ambassadors should be fully briefed and energized
- Visual content, storytelling, and leadership visibility all matter
- Tease the message in advance to build anticipation
- Monitor in real time and be ready to adjust your messaging based on feedback

Treat your launch as a moment worth remembering, not just announcing. You are selling hope for the future.

Final Thought

Opening Day is not just a date on the calendar, it is a declaration. It tells your fans, your opponents, and your own clubhouse exactly who you intend to be this season. Momentum does not arrive by chance. It is built in the first moments when you take the field with purpose.

Back in the office, any change is worthy of its own Opening Day. Your audience is watching closely, deciding whether to trust you, follow you, and invest in what you offer. Before you speak a word, they read your confidence, your preparation, and your belief in what you are presenting.

Step into that moment with conviction. Bring the pride, precision, and energy that tells everyone you are here to compete and here to stay. Because when you open strong, you do more than start the game, you set the tone for every inning that follows.

First impressions are not just introductions. They set the tone of the mission. Start strong, lead with energy, and deliver your message with confidence. Whether speaking to internal or external audiences, a powerful first impression builds momentum and carries you toward the win.

🎬 Movie Break: A League of Their Own 🎬

Resilience, Redefining the Rules, and Competing with Heart

Baseball Principle

"It's supposed to be hard. If it wasn't hard, everyone would do it. The hard is what makes it great." This iconic line from Rockford Peaches manager Jimmy Dugan, played by Tom Hanks, is more than a pep talk. It is a truth about leadership, excellence, and growth.

Set during World War II, *A League of Their Own* tells the story of the All-American Girls Professional Baseball League, a pioneering group of women who stepped onto the diamond when male athletes were called to war. These women were expected to fail, to falter, or at best, to simply hold the place until baseball could return to the way it was.

Instead, they competed with skill, dignity, and unmatched heart. They won games, drew crowds, and changed minds.

At the center of the story is Dottie Hinson, a gifted catcher who never asked to lead, but became the team's anchor. Alongside her are teammates, including her stubborn sister and pitcher Kit, all with grit, quirks, doubts, and dreams. Each player in the league battles personal struggles and societal expectations, but together they prove that passion, discipline, and teamwork can shatter any barrier.

This is not just a baseball story. It is a leadership case study.

Business Strategy

Just like in the film, the rules are not always fair in business. Leaders are often judged more by perception than by performance. Professionals are asked to meet unspoken expectations, manage images, and deliver results while walking a tightrope of visibility and scrutiny.

Dottie Hinson embodies the reluctant leader many professionals become. She does not seek attention, but her talent makes her a focal point. She leads not with bravado, but with calm execution. Others follow her because she shows up consistently, performs under pressure, and supports her team when it counts.

Leadership in business often looks like Peaches' star catcher. It is not about having the most boisterous voice in the room. It is about delivering when it matters, building trust with quiet integrity, and carrying others when they lose their footing.

At the same time, the women in the league were held to a double standard. They had to play well, look polished, and constantly prove they belonged. This mirrors today's world of 24/7 visibility where leaders are judged on performance and image simultaneously.

The Rockford Peaches did not just play the game. They redefined it by fighting through prejudice and adversity. That is a playbook every modern leader should study.

Real-World Example

In *A League of Their Own*, the Rockford Peaches were told to smile while sliding into bases, wear skirts while diving for line drives, and entertain crowds while playing championship-caliber baseball. They had to prove they belonged by excelling on the field while performing under rules designed to hold them back.

That tension still exists in today's workplace. Many leaders feel they must play two games at once by excelling at their craft while managing how others perceive them. They are asked to deliver results while also meeting standards of appearance, tone, or style that their peers are not held to.

Consider a young female executive stepping into her first senior leadership role. She knows the mission, drives revenue, leads teams, manages growth, but quickly realizes she is also being judged on presence, appearance, and whether she is too confident or not confident enough. Like Hinson, she did not ask to carry that weight, but she shoulders it with grace. She learns to lead with calm execution, to bring her team together in tense moments, and to let consistent results speak louder than perception.

Her story mirrors the Peaches. The scoreboard may not capture the extra pressures, but every breakthrough victory, every promotion earned, and every barrier broken is more than personal success. It is a step forward for those who will follow.

Business Tip

When building your professional presence and leadership brand in a competitive, high-visibility environment, consider these strategies:

- Focus on substance before spotlight, your performance will earn attention naturally
- Stay centered on values, especially when expectations feel unfair
- Let consistency be your voice when others question your presence
- Share the credit with the team, even when the spotlight is on you
- Lead with care, clarity, and confidence that comes from doing the work well

You do not need to prove everything to everyone. Lead your way and let the results speak.

Final Thought

A League of Their Own reminds us that the road to greatness is rarely smooth. It is filled with long bus rides to small towns, playing through aching muscles, and stepping onto the field knowing some people are rooting for you to fail. It is the sting of doubt when your own teammates question your place, and the pressure of proving yourself in a world that is not yet ready to see you win.

The women of the Rockford Peaches did not just play baseball, they broke barriers. They faced jeers from the stands, skepticism from the press, and the strain of leaving families behind. Yet they led with heart, committed to their craft, and carried one another through every inning. Their victories were not just in the box score. They were in every young girl who watched them and realized the game could be theirs too.

That is the power of leading with courage and conviction. You do more than win games, you change the standard, you change the story, and you change the game itself.

The hard is what makes it great. It is what forged Dottie's quiet strength, Kit's resilience, and the unshakable bond between teammates who became family. When you rise to that challenge, when you push through the grind, the doubt, and the noise, you do not just lead, you win.

You inspire others to believe that they can lead too. Real leadership is not about standing apart from your team. It is about standing with your team, sliding into home, dirt on your uniform, and knowing that you all have left all you had out on the field together.

⚾ Section 3: Adaptability ⚾

21

You're Only as Good as Your Farm System – Mentorship & Nurturing Talent

Building the Next Generation Before You Need Them

Baseball Principle

In Major League Baseball, dynasties are not built on talent alone, they are built on depth. A great starting lineup may win a game. However, a great farm system creates a successful franchise with plenty of talent in the pipeline ready to sustain a winning culture for years.

Take the Atlanta Braves of the 1990s and early 2000s. Their prolonged success came not only from Hall of Famers like Chipper Jones, Tom Glavine, and John Smoltz, but from a robust pipeline of young talent that was developed, tested, and ready to contribute. Similarly, the Houston Astros playoff resurgence was powered by years of farm system investment, cultivating stars like Carlos Correa, Jose Altuve, and Alex Bregman long before their names were known outside of spring training.

For MLB franchises, the minor league farm system is not an afterthought. It is the foundation. It absorbs injuries, trades, slumps, and replaces panic with readiness. It signals an organization that thinks, not just about today's game, but about playing baseball in October. Behind every big-league breakthrough is a long runway of coaching, growth, and preparation. That is where legacies are built.

Business Strategy

In the traditional business environment, your farm system is the people you are cultivating to lead when their moment comes. Whether you call it mentorship, professional development, or succession planning, the goal is the same. Effective organizations need to develop tomorrow's leaders before they need them.

When companies ignore this, they find themselves scrambling when a key leader leaves, retires, or burns out. Transition becomes turmoil. When succession is intentional, and mentoring is cultural, the handoff feels natural and smooth. The organization stays focused. The mission stays intact.

Great companies do not leave leadership development to chance. They identify high-potential talent early, pair them with mentors, and give them meaningful responsibilities before the spotlight is on them. Leadership is not a surprise promotion but a cultivated readiness. Your farm system is not a luxury. It is your lifeline.

Real-World Example

A rapidly growing consulting firm had earned national recognition, but inside its walls a quiet challenge was looming. Three founding executives, each central to client relationships and daily operations, had all planned to retire within two years. For many firms, that kind of transition could have been destabilizing, even threatening to undo years of progress.

The leadership team refused to wait until the crisis arrived. Instead, they launched Project Legacy, an internal initiative designed to build leadership depth before it was desperately needed. Rising managers were nominated by their peers and invited into an intensive 6-month rotation. They worked side by side with senior leaders on real client projects, budget planning, and high-stakes proposals. Monthly mentorship meetings are paired with seasoned wisdom with fresh perspectives. At the program's midpoint, participants were tested in crisis simulations, making tough calls under pressure and defending their reasoning to executives who had weathered decades of challenges.

By the end of the program, each manager had a personal growth plan co-created with a mentor, a roadmap that was as practical as it was inspiring. When the first retirement finally came, there was no scramble. The successor had already been quietly leading, shadowing responsibilities, and earning trust. To clients, the change was seamless. To the firm, it was proof that continuity could be built. Not by chance, but by deliberate investment in people.

That is what a modern farm system looks like, steady, intentional, and deeply human. It is leadership not as a reaction, but as a legacy in motion.

Business Tip

To build a farm system that secures your organization's future:

- Identify critical roles and assess who could grow into them over time
- Pair rising talent with mentors in structured and intentional ways
- Include leadership exposure in development with shadowing, presentations, decision-making
- Crosstrain across departments to build versatility and institutional memory
- Normalize development conversations by making succession planning part of the culture, not a taboo concept

A thriving farm system creates momentum, reduces risk, and inspires loyalty.

Final Thought

The roar of the crowd may follow the big-league stars, but real work and growth happen far from the spotlight in the minor leagues throughout all levels of the organization. That is where players are molded, where resilience is tested, and where the habits of greatness take root. Whether you are playing for the Winter Garden Squeeze in the Florida Collegiate Summer League or on the international stage representing your country in the Tokyo Dome for the World Baseball Classic, your pipeline matters.

Your true legacy will not be measured by what you achieved alone, but by the people you lifted, the leaders you nurtured, and the culture you left behind. Do not wait until your starters are gone to notice the strength of your bench. Start now developing talent in your business. Invest in their growth. Share your game plan. Give your talent chances to lead before they feel ready.

Someday, you will not take the field. However, it will be someone you coached, empowered, and believed in before they ever wore the uniform. When that day comes, you will not have to hope they are ready. You will know because you prepared them for success.

Great leaders do not just win on their own. They plan to set up victories long before they leave the field. Let your legacy be the team that thrives because you chose to prepare them for a game you will never play. Let your legacy live on through the leaders you empower.

22

Designated Hitters Deliver – Specialists Who Make a Big Impact

Knowing When to Rely on Your Team's Focused Expertise

Baseball Principle

The designated hitter (DH) may not play in the field, but his presence in the lineup changes everything. Introduced to the American League in 1973, the DH role allowed teams to insert a power bat for the pitcher without sacrificing defense. The DH is now standard across all Major League Baseball when it was additionally adopted by the National League in 2022. Feared Hall of Fame DHs like Edgar Martínez and Frank Thomas made careers out of it. They delivered clutch hits, walk-off home runs, and moments that defined eras and solidified their Hall of Fame memberships.

Thomas was legendary in his role. Known as The Big Hurt, while playing some first base, he was his team's top offensive producer for a generation. When the Chicago White Sox needed a hit to change a game or carry a season, he stepped to the plate and delivered. Time and again, Thomas showed that his power, patience, and presence could tilt the outcome with a single swing.

The DH is not asked to do everything. He is asked to do one thing, exceptionally. That kind of focus makes the difference between playing the game and winning it. There is deep wisdom in knowing which players shine brightest when you let them stay in their genius zone.

Business Strategy

Modern workplaces often celebrate flexibility, and rightly so in small businesses. Many team members wear multiple hats, juggle roles, and adapt to changing demands. Some situations demand a different kind of contribution with specialized precision.

When a major decision hangs on the accuracy of your analytics, you call the data expert. When a new brand is being born, you bring in a creative designer who understands nuance and emotion. When a reputational risk threatens your organization, you don't crowdsource the message, you call the communicator who has been through the fire.

These are your designated hitters as they may not attend every meeting. They may not be part of the weekly routine. However, when it is time to deliver, when the stakes are high, they swing with impact.

Great leaders build teams with range, but they also know when to concentrate on talent. Specialists are not just a luxury. They are often the difference-makers in securing victory.

Real World Example

A lobbying firm was retained by a coalition facing a make-or-break legislative session. The client group had passion and expertise in their field, but they lacked the bandwidth and political reach to navigate the state Capitol under pressure.

The firm moved quickly. They studied the landscape, identified key committee chairs, and built a message framework that spoke to both sides of the political aisle. They drafted concise briefing packets tailored for lawmakers, secured earned media placements that framed the issue in favorable terms, and aligned a digital strategy with legislative milestones so the public conversation reinforced the lobbying effort.

By the time the bill hit the floor, momentum was on their side. Legislators referenced the firm's talking points in debate, coverage appeared in statewide outlets, and the coalition's position gained bipartisan support.

The lobbying firm didn't become a permanent extension of the client's staff, but in the moments that mattered most, they were the designated hitter. They stepped in, swinging with purpose, and changing the outcome of the game.

Business Tip

To make the most of your specialists:

- Know when precision matters more than versatility
- Keep a trusted list of freelancers, consultants, or advisors you can activate
- Don't dilute the impact by pulling specialists into non-essential tasks
- Help your team understand why and when specialists are brought in
- Make them feel like part of the team, even if only for a few at-bats

A well-used specialist does not slow you down, as they make your entire team better.

Final Thought

The designated hitter may have one purpose, but at the right moment that purpose makes game changing impact. One trip up to the plate. One pitch. One swing. The entire momentum of the game shifts. The DH is not there to do everything. He is there to get a hit, to drive home the run when it matters most.

Back in the office, success often comes down to the same truth. You do not need everyone to be good at everything. You need the right person, with the right skill, stepping in at exactly the right time. Specialists bring focus. They bring mastery. When the stakes are high, they bring results that no one else can deliver.

Build your roster with care. Let your generalists keep the organization moving but when the big inning comes, do not hesitate. Put your specialist up to the plate. Clear the noise. Let them swing and perform their specialty.

Sometimes, everything rides on that one moment. When it does, the win goes to the leader who trusted the right person to deliver it. Send in the DH. Trust their skill. Give them space. Let them swing because that one hit might be the one that wins it all.

23

Utility Players Win Games – Cross-Functional Agility

Versatility Creates Value in Fast-Moving Environments

Baseball Principle

The DH is a required specialist. However, in the 162-game season, the true test of a baseball team is not just in its stars but in its team depth. That's where the utility player becomes a difference-maker. Teams need the right player at the right time in the right role.

Players like Ben Zobrist, Jose Oquendo, and even all-time MLB hits leader Pete Rose have built careers not dominating one position, but by mastering many. Zobrist, for instance, played every position except pitcher and catcher during his career and was instrumental in the Chicago Cubs' 2016 World Series win, earning MVP honors for his steady, clutch performance.

The utility player is the glue guy. He does not seek the attention but is always ready. Over the course of a week, he can play second base in the afternoon, left field the next evening, and pinch-hit when the pressure is highest. His mindset is simple, wherever the team needs him, he will go.

He is not defined by the stat sheet but by trust, versatility, and reliability. In the long grind of the baseball season, that adaptability can mean the difference between holding the line or falling apart. He is the player you lean on when the moment matters most, because he never tries to be anything other than exactly what the team needs

Business Strategy

There are utility players in every organization. The professionals who may not always stand in the pressure cooker but keep the game moving forward. They are the ones who step into gaps without hesitation, wear multiple hats without complaint, and never fall back on the phrase, that's not my job.

Think about the marketer who not only builds campaigns but also learns the client's technical product well enough to explain it in plain language. Or the operations lead who can shift from managing logistics to selling strategy in front of a board. Or the executive assistant who, when a crisis hits, suddenly becomes the project manager who keeps deadlines on track. Their value does not lie in narrow specialization. It lies in their agility, initiative, and willingness to step up wherever the team needs them most.

In today's fast-moving business environment, these cross-functional players bring stability when the pace quickens. They reduce friction when priorities collide. They keep execution alive when resources are thin and roles are unclear. You may not always notice them in the headlines or the annual report, but when challenges mount, they are the ones who make sure the work never stops.

They are not flashy, but they are indispensable. When things get chaotic, they do not freeze, because they can flex in any role. That ability is what turns potential breakdowns into breakthroughs.

Real-World Example

A state university was preparing for its first major curriculum overhaul in decades. The stakes were high. Faculty input needed to be heard, accreditation requirements had to be met, and the release date was tied to a public announcement from the university president.

Departments worked in silos. The English faculty had not spoken with the science department in months. Student affairs were unaware of the new requirements being proposed in numerous academic departments. Tensions were mounting. Deadlines loomed.

That is when a junior academic advisor, originally hired to help students with course selection, stepped up like a true utility player. They volunteered to attend cross-department curriculum meetings, jumped in to manage scheduling conflicts, and connected faculty who did not realize they were working on overlapping courses. They took on communications with the registrar, joined calls, coordinated student feedback, and even handled last-minute adjustments to the collective university plan.

They did not have a senior title, but their willingness to play multiple roles, switching seamlessly between strategist, communicator, and coordinator, but ultimately kept the overhaul on schedule. When the updated curriculum launched without delays, the dean credited their adaptability and teamwork as a key reason for the success. Today after a promotion, the junior academic advisor leads a cross-college working group that continues to strengthen communication across departments.

Business Tip

To empower utility players in your organization:

- Create stretch opportunities that allow people to work outside their core role
- Encourage shadowing and department rotations to build broader perspective
- Reward adaptability and initiative, not just task completion
- Build teams that pair specialists with generalists for balanced execution
- Recognize leadership in unlikely places as utility players often influence culture more than titleholders

Versatility is not an organization's Plan B. It is a strategic asset to put the right people in the right place, at the right time.

Final Thought

The utility player in baseball rarely makes the headlines. They are not the first name on the lineup card or the one splashed across the highlight reel. When a starter goes down, when the infield needs reshuffling, or when a playoff game teeters on a single play, they are the ones the manager calls. They step into any position, any role, and deliver exactly what the moment demands.

The same truth holds in any organization. Utility players are the ones who bridge departments, calm tensions, and keep projects alive when chaos threatens to take over. They adapt without complaint. They lead without ego. They know that success is not about personal credit, as it is about keeping the team in the game.

Do not underestimate the quiet force of adaptability. Recognize it. Reward it. Build it into your culture. Give these players the tools, trust, and freedom to use their versatility, and they will repay you tenfold.

When the pressure peaks and you are down to your last out, it is not always the star who secures the win. It is the one who was prepared for any role, at any moment. The teammate who stays ready becomes the difference-maker when the game is on the line.

Baseball and business are similar as the season is often saved not by the one who does the most spectacular thing, but by the one who is prepared to do whatever is needed. Be the kind of leader who sees in value in diversity, team flexibility, and never lets them sit idle when the game is on the line.

24

Play the Waiver Wire – Hiring & Freelance Strategy

Smart Talent Acquisition at the Right Time for the Right Role

Baseball Principle

In Major League Baseball, the waiver wire is where the sharpest general managers make quiet moves that lead to results. It is a tool for teams willing to think creatively and act quickly. A struggling veteran gets released. A journeyman infielder becomes available. A high-upside prospect is designated for assignment to the minor leagues. For the unprepared, these moments pass unnoticed. However, for the alert general management team with a vision, they are golden opportunities.

Before becoming a postseason legend, Randy Arozarena was considered expendable. He was designated for assignment by the St. Louis Cardinals and was picked up by Tampa Bay. Yet with the Rays, he set the all-time MLB record with 10 postseason home runs in 2020, proving that greatness can emerge from the most overlooked places.

At the time, Arozarena was not a marquee name, but he was the perfect piece at the perfect moment. Depth wins often with unsung heroes. Depth is built through strategy by filling in the gaps when the need arises. Finding the diamond in the rough is not luck, but strategy.

Business Strategy

Making a new hire often comes as a reaction to a problem as someone leaves, a project grows, a deadline moves up. The results often end in scramble mode. Rushed hiring processes, overextended teams, and reactive decisions that cost more in the long run.

Smart organizations do it differently. They play their version of the waiver wire. Every decision is based on calm strategic moves.

They build relationships with freelancers, consultants, and part-time specialists before the pressure hits. They scout platforms, attend industry events, and keep an open eye for emerging talent sometimes even when no open role exists. They treat contingent labor not as a compromise but as a strategic extension of their team.

This approach gives them agility. When an unexpected injury comes, they do not panic. They plug in the right person, at the right time, for the right role and the work keeps moving forward. Talent is not just about who you hire full-time. It is about who you can call when it matters.

Real-World Example

In a small media market in a college town, a local television station faced a make-or-break moment. The town's centennial celebration was approaching, a once-in-a-generation event that would draw thousands of visitors and the attention of state media. The station wanted to provide wall-to-wall coverage, but budget constraints and a lean staff left them stretched thin.

The station's news director had a solution. Over the past few years, they had quietly built relationships with a network of community contributors with retired journalists, aspiring videographers from the local college, and bilingual reporters trusted in underserved neighborhoods. These connections were nurtured long before the big event, through coffee meetings, small collaborations, and regular check-ins.

When the centennial arrived, the station was ready. Contributors provided on-the-ground footage from every corner of the celebration. Interviews aired in English and Spanish. Human-interest stories poured in from community contacts who might otherwise have been overlooked.

The coverage was so comprehensive and personal that viewership spiked, advertising revenue exceeded projections, and the station earned recognition from the state broadcasters' association. This success was merely luck because it was the result of preparation, relationship-building, and knowing exactly who to call when the spotlight turned on.

Business Tip

To build your own version of the waiver wire:

- Track freelancers, contractors, and former collaborators you trust
- Give specialists micro-projects to assess their fit before committing to larger work
- Attending industry events not just to learn, but to scout talent
- Templates, onboarding checklists, and clear scopes accelerate activation
- When freelance work is treated as strategic, quality follows throughout the team

The best hires are not always the splashiest. Sometimes they are just the timeliest.

Final Thought

Championships are not always decided by the biggest stars. Sometimes they hinge on the free agent player you signed during the season. The one who came in quietly, hit a clutch double, turned a game-saving double play, or simply brought a new energy that lifted the entire clubhouse.

The same truth applies in business. The right person at the right time can shift the momentum of an entire project, department, or organization. Those leaders who seem to get lucky with talent are not relying on chance. These leaders are always looking, always networking, always building relationships before the need is urgent.

Proactive organizations do not wait for a staffing crisis to start searching. Leaders do not leave their next big win to chance, so they scan the wire. They keep the bench warm. They invest in conversations and connections today, that may become their difference-makers tomorrow.

A single smart team pickup can change the outcome of the season. A well-timed call can rescue a project and preserve a quarter. When that opportunity comes, leaders who are ready do not hesitate, they make the move that everyone else wishes they had made first. Recognize when the right opportunity comes along and make your move.

25

Golden Glove Protection – Risk Management & Quality Control

Play Precision Defense to Protect Reputations, Resources, and Results

Baseball Principle

The Gold Glove is baseball's highest recognition for defensive excellence. These plays may not lead the highlight reels the way home runs do, but when the game is on the line, you want the Gold Glove player handling the ball. Defense may look unassuming, but it is what holds championships together.

Think of shortstop Ozzie Smith, nicknamed "The Wizard," whose backflips were dazzling but whose glove work was even more amazing. Or the Baltimore Orioles' Brooks Robinson, whose ability to play the hot corner at third base saved countless runs. These were players who made the extraordinary look routine, and the spectacular look flawless, with Smith winning career 13 Gold Gloves and Robinson with 16. However interestingly enough, the record is 18 belonging to Hall of Famer Greg Maddux, a pitcher.

Gold Glove winners do not chase headlines. They eliminate risk. They turn hits into outs and routine plays into consistent victories. When a game teeters on the edge, it is often a perfect pivot at shortstop or a dug-out scoop at first that keeps hope alive.

In the postseason, where every pitch matters, great defense is not a bonus, it is a necessity. A misplayed grounder can cost the season. A game-saving dive in the field for an out can secure a championship.

Business Strategy

Your Gold Glove defenders are not usually the ones designing products or speaking at press conferences. They are the ones checking the footnotes, vetting the legal language, ensuring brand consistency, verifying facts, and running the final review. They are your quality control.

They may not be front-and-center in your strategy sessions, but they are critical to your success. Risk in business is rarely explosive, it is accumulative. A misused phrase in a press release. A wrong logo in a partner presentation. An outdated statistic in a government graphic. These details may seem small, but they have big consequences.

Organizations that value precision build systems that protect them. They do not fear mistakes, as they prepare for them. They assign ownership. They rehearse their defense. They run drills in the form of quality control workflows, checklists, and scenario planning. Good defense keeps great work from being undone by small errors.

Real-World Example

A health agency was in the final week of launching a campaign aimed at increasing vaccinations among vulnerable populations. The campaign had broad reach, social, print, radio, and local transportation. Everything was on schedule.

During final review, a quality assurance lead, a former nurse turned communications specialist, noticed a footnote on one of the print ads that referenced an obsolete dosage recommendation. It was a small text box and easy to miss.

Had the campaign gone live, it would have conflicted with updated federal guidelines, risking public confusion, media backlash, and political scrutiny. The team had built in a second-layer quality assurance process and empowered someone to speak candidly. The content was corrected, redistributed, and launched without reputational damage.

No applause. No headlines. However, that moment preserved the campaign and the agency's credibility. That is what Golden Glove protection looks like in action.

Business Tip

To elevate your defensive strategy:

- Establish a multi-layered review system, especially for public-facing content
- Assign ownership of final quality control and compliance on every project
- Maintain an up-to-date risk register that tracks project vulnerabilities
- Invest in training with legal, branding, and regulatory literacy across teams
- Celebrate detail-oriented professionals who prevent problems, not just fix them

Your defense should be quietly relentless, not occasionally reactive.

Final Thought

Every championship team needs a slugger who can clear the bases with one swing. They also need the second baseman who never boots the routine grounder, the player who makes quiet and dependable plays that keep the team in position to win.

The same holds true in business. It is easy to celebrate the big contracts, the growth charts, and the headline-grabbing achievements. Behind every moment of glory is a layer of protection, a process, or a habit that ensures nothing vital slips through the cracks.

Build a culture that plays clean. Value the detail-keepers who catch mistakes before they snowball into crises. Celebrate the people who take pride in the small, unseen wins that protect the big, visible ones.

Because when the lights are bright and the pressure is high, it is not just the heavy hitters who win the game. It is the sure-handed defender you trust to make the play when it matters most. Quality defense is truly golden.

In life, that trust is built long before the spotlight hits. It comes from preparation, discipline, and pride in doing the little things right every time. Play clean. Play smart. Protect the win and you will find yourself winning more than games, you will be building something rooted in quality with a legacy that lasts.

26

Pinch Hit When Needed – Agile Leadership Under Pressure

Step In, Step Up, and Deliver When the Moment Demands It

Baseball Principle

In the final innings of a tight game, the manager looks down the bench, for a pinch hitter in a strategic clutch moment. Some players have been waiting the whole game, watching from the bench, tracking pitchers, and staying warm. They may not have taken a swing in a live game in days, but now the game rests on what they can do next.

Addison Barger commands attention as the only player in history to hit a pinch hit grand slam home run in the World Series, who cemented his legacy with a clutch blast for the Toronto Blue Jays in 2025. However, Lenny Harris built his entire career in baseball through consistency and readiness. He didn't earn this reputation through the fanfare of home runs, but he did go 1-4 pinch hitting in the World Series for the Florida Marlins championship in 2003.

Harris was not routinely in the everyday lineup, nor was he a perennial All-Star. Instead, he made his legacy as baseball's top pinch hitter. He carved out a niche that required patience, poise, and perfect timing with 212 career pinch hits for eight MLB teams. He became the player managers keep in reserve for the exact moment when the game's outcome hinged on a single swing.

The role of the pinch hitter is uniquely challenging. Without the timing of regular at-bats during the game, they must step into the box cold. Often against a fresh closer or a dominant starter deep into the game. There is no warmup inning, no gradual feel for the strike zone, just an immediate, high-pressure confrontation. They meet that challenge with preparation in the dugout, studying pitchers, staying loose, and keeping his timing sharp so he could be ready on a moment's notice.

Pinch hitters don't get the everyday spots in the starting lineups. They don't usually get glory. When the spotlight hits them, they are ready. They stay mentally engaged. They know the game situation they are entering. They read the pitcher. When their name is called, they walk to the plate like they've been in the lineup the whole game. That's the power of preparation without attention, being ready when no one's watching, and rising to the challenge when everyone is looking.

Business Strategy

Every organization eventually faces a high-pressure moment, the keynote speaker cancels the night before, a critical client changes direction mid-project, or a core team member calls out sick just hours before a deadline.

In those moments, titles and organizational charts do not matter. What matters is who can step in, steady the team, and deliver in the clutch. Agile leaders prepare for these moments long before they arrive. They pay attention to details outside their lane. They learn the workflows. They understand the client's expectations. They stay close enough to the action, if called upon, they can step up without hesitation.

When the unexpected happens, pinch hitters in business do not panic. They step forward with a don't worry I've got this confidence, then follow through with calm skill. They are not chasing the spotlight. They are protecting the win.

Their value is not measured only by the work they do every day, but by the gap they are willing and able to fill when the team needs them most. Sometimes the most important play you make is not the one you were hired. But the one you were ready for.

Real-World Example

At a digital application firm, a high-profile product presentation was set to debut during a nationally televised awards show. Months of planning had gone into the campaign, advertising buys, influencer partnerships, and a coordinated social media rollout timed to the minute.

The morning of the launch, disaster struck. The project's lead account manager was sidelined by a health emergency. The team was rattled. Key details about final creative approvals, media contact lists, and event-day talking points were locked in their head.

That is when a senior copywriter, someone whose official role was far from campaign logistics, stepped in. They had been quietly following the project's progress, asking questions during meetings, and offering to proofread materials. Because of this, they already knew the timeline, the media plan, and the client's voice.

They made calls to confirm ad placement, coordinated with the production crew to ensure assets were delivered on time, and even jumped into the live event's media center to handle last-minute interview requests. The launch not only went ahead without delay, but it also exceeded engagement targets by 20 percent.

When the dust settled, the client never even knew there had been a crisis. The pinch hitter had done their job. However, in the process, they learned the hard way of documenting everything and keeping someone on the bench in the clutch.

Business Tip

Every organization needs to develop their own go-to pinch hitters:

- Don't just master your lane, understand the wider field
- Even when you're not leading, absorb how decisions get made
- Know where to find what others may forget
- Practice presenting, troubleshooting, and stepping in
- Raise your hand for stretch projects as they build confidence and visibility

Leadership is not about waiting your turn. It is about being ready when the turn comes early.

Final Thought

The pinch hitter's name might not be on the marquee outside of the stadium. They might not have had a single at-bat all game. When the lights are bright, the crowd is roaring, and the game is on the line, the pinch hitter steps up with poise, precision, and purpose.

It is no different being off the diamond. Some of the most defining moments come from people who were not in the game yet, who chose to take charge when the moment demanded it. They were ready because they had been watching, listening, and learning long before anyone called their name.

Leadership is not about always being at center stage. It is about being ready when the team needs you. Stay sharp. Stay alert. Study the signals. Know the playbook well enough to step in cold and still deliver under pressure.

When the call comes, walk to the plate with a calm, cool, and collected attitude. Trust the preparation you have done behind the scenes. Swing with confidence, not hesitation. In the leadership game, you may only get one swing and the leaders who make it count are remembered long after the game is over.

27

On Deck and Ready – Team Readiness & Professional Development

Prepare Your People Before the Moment Arrives

Baseball Principle

The on-deck circle is not a place of silent waiting. It is a place of intentional game preparation. As the next man up to bat, the one in the on-deck circle up grips the bat, watches the pitcher's delivery, adjusts their stance, and visualizes their at-bat. They are not in the box yet, but they are already in the game, mentally, physically, and emotionally.

Some of baseball's most clutch performances began in the on-deck circle, where players studied every detail so they could seize their moment. When future Hall of Famer Carlton Fisk stepped to the plate in the 12th inning of Game 6 of the 1975 World Series, the Red Sox were fighting to stay alive against the Reds. He had been locked in all night, tracking pitches, anticipating his chance. Watching. Timing. Trusting. When he got the pitch he wanted, he made it count, sending it high over the Green Monster in Fenway Park, waving it fair, and etching his name and this iconic moment into baseball history forever.

Being on deck is not idle. It is readiness with intention. Great players are not surprised by opportunity, because they are prepared for it.

Business Strategy

In too many organizations, people wait until the promotion is announced, the seat is vacated, or the crisis hits to prepare for leadership. The most resilient teams are built on constant readiness where being on deck is not about hierarchy, but about mindset.

An on-deck culture means emerging leaders are being developed before they are needed. They're given visibility into strategic thinking, mentored through shadow roles, and invited to contribute beyond their title. They learn not just by doing but by being present in the moments that matter.

Organizations that prioritize readiness don't scramble when change comes. They rotate players in with confidence because they've already been in the dugout, watching the game unfold. Great leadership is not built in the moment. It's built before the moment.

Real-World Example

At a busy hospital, the leadership team faced an urgent challenge. The lead nurse coordinator for a high-priority patient safety initiative took another job across the country just weeks before a major accreditation review. The project couldn't stall deadlines, as compliance requirements, and patient care protocols were already set in motion.

The team didn't panic. A staff nurse, only three years out of school, had spent the past year volunteering for quality improvement committees, shadowing the coordinator during planning sessions, and completing advanced training modules on their own time. They asked questions, learned workflows, and built relationships across departments so they could see the big picture.

When the vacancy opened, they stepped in without hesitation. Within days, they were leading safety briefings, coordinating cross-unit checklists, and presenting readiness updates to hospital leadership. The initiative stayed on track, the review passed with high marks, and their promotion to a permanent leadership role followed soon after. That's what being on deck, and staying ready, looks like in an organization.

Business Tip

To cultivate a strong on-deck culture in your organization:

- Invite high-potential employees to observe senior-level meetings and strategic planning
- Establish rotating leadership roles that allow team members to stretch into new skill sets
- Build learning into daily work and make development proactive, not reactive
- Give feedback early and often and help your people grow before they're tested
- Recognize preparation as performance and not just output, but ownership

If you wait until someone is needed to prepare them, you've waited too long.

Final Thought

The player in the on-deck circle isn't just standing there waiting. He is analyzing the moment, watching the movement of each pitch, noting the quirks of the pitcher's windup, the release point, and different speeds. His hands are on the bat, but his mind is already in the batter's box, rehearsing his swing in every detail as if his turn had already arrived. By the time he hears his name called, he isn't scrambling to get ready, he is simply stepping into the role he has been preparing for all along.

Your next leader may not have the title, the office, or the formal authority, but the signs are already there if you are paying attention. They are the ones learning in the background, taking on extra assignments, asking thoughtful questions in meetings, and seeking out mentorship without being prompted. They are building relationships, expanding their knowledge, and putting in the quiet work long before the spotlight ever finds them.

Great teams are not built solely on the all-stars in the lineup. They are built on people who believe their opportunity will come and who act with intention and readiness every day. These are the individuals who step in without hesitation when the unexpected happens, whether that means replacing an injured starter in the bottom of the ninth or filling a critical leadership gap in the middle of a high-stakes project.

If you want your organization to thrive in the long run, you must be able to spot the ones who are already in their own on-deck circle, studying, preparing, and positioning themselves to contribute when it matters most. Give them opportunities to grow, challenge them with real responsibility, and show them that their readiness is valued. The future of your success is not just out on the field today, it's also standing just a few steps away, waiting for the signal to step up and take their swing.

28

Seventh-Inning Stretch – Recharging & Preventing Burnout

Pause with Purpose to Maintain Peak Performance

Baseball Principle

The seventh-inning stretch is more than a break in the game. It is sacred tradition within baseball. After six full and a half innings of strategy, stress, and stamina, players and fans alike rise to breathe, reset, and rally for the final push. The crackle of the crowd shifts to harmony as voices join together in the familiar anthem of *Take Me Out to the Ball Game.*

In Chicago's Wrigley Field, that moment became iconic for generations of fans. The legendary Hall of Fame Cub's play by play announcer Harry Caray, with arms held out wide and voice booming through the loudspeaker, turned the seventh inning stretch into a celebration. It was joy, nostalgia, and community wrapped into one simple song. Behind the fun was something vital, a collective breath, a moment of togetherness that reminded everyone why they showed up.

Even though the seventh-inning stretch has become more noteworthy for the fans, players and the coaches also regroup. How you emerge from that stretch break often determines the outcome of the game. Rest is not weakness. It is part of the game plan.

Business Strategy

A proverbial seventh-inning stretch is often skipped in today's work culture. The pace of business rarely pauses. Deadlines stack up, meetings bleed into each other and reading all the unread emails have become a warped badge of honor. Teams push through without stopping, mistaking constant intensity for commitment. Just as in baseball, playing every inning at full speed without a reset does not build endurance. It drains it.

Great leaders recognize that sustainable performance requires recovery. A project team that pauses to regroup, recalibrate, and breathe is not wasting time. They are building capacity to finish strong. A culture that encourages employees to take real vacations, to step away without guilt, or to recharge during the day creates more focus and better outcomes when it matters most.

Conceptualize the seventh-inning stretch not as a break from the game, but as an integral part of the game. It is the reset that allows players to dig deep for the final innings. In the same way, organizations that embrace purposeful pauses set themselves up for comebacks, breakthroughs, and big wins. Leaders who build this strategy into their culture protect not just performance but also people, ensuring clarity, collaboration, and creativity last until the very end.

Real-World Example

A technology startup had built a reputation for hustle. Their products were innovative, their client list impressive, but signs of strain were showing. Teams worked late, turnover increased, and innovation slowed. Leadership noticed the slump, but instead of pushing harder, they pulled back.

They introduced a quarterly Innovation Day, a no-meeting, no-deliverable day where employees were free to brainstorm, explore ideas, or just take a breath. They also added a two-day summer company-wide closure and formalized end-of-day check-out rituals.

These efforts resulted in a productivity rebound. More patents were filed. Retention improved and employees reported a stronger sense of purpose. The seventh-inning stretch had arrived, not as a break from work, but as a critical part of how they worked. Like Harry Caray leading a crowd in song, recharging should be joyful, a moment that reconnects people to the mission, to each other, and to themselves.

Business Tip

To build a sustainable, high-performing culture that avoids burnout and finishes strong:

- Schedule purposeful pauses that are built into team calendars, not just taken when people are exhausted
- Normalize rest as a necessary part of peak performance and reinforce that excellence includes recovery
- Encourage team members to take PTO without guilt and model that behavior from leadership
- Use casual surveys and regular check-ins to monitor team morale and identify fatigue before it becomes burnout
- Integrate moments of fun, reflection, and celebration that restore energy and remind teams why their work matters

Rest is not a retreat. It is a strategy, and the best teams know how to use it.

Final Thought

When Harry Caray leaned out of the Wrigley Field broadcast booth and led thousands of fans in *Take Me Out to the Ball Game.* He wasn't just filling a seventh-inning tradition, he was giving people a shared experience. For a few minutes, the scoreboard didn't matter. The strikeouts and errors faded. Everyone, players, coaches, fans, had permission to smile, to sing off-key, and to remember why they loved being at the ballpark in the first place.

Your team needs that same kind of space. Not once a year at a holiday party but routine breaks built into the fabric of your work. A steady beat of restoration that says to your team they are valued for their well-being as much as their performance. Burnout rarely arrives with fireworks. It slips in unnoticed when we skip the stretch, when we sprint from one high-stakes inning to the next without pausing to catch our breath.

As a leader, it's your job to create those moments of reprieve. To call time when the pace gets relentless. To encourage a laugh in the middle of a deadline. To remind people that passion is sustained not by constant motion, but by balance. Just like a team that huddles between innings, your organization's resilience is built in brief, but intentional, pauses.

The best leaders understand that the journey to victory isn't one long marathon. It's a series of innings, each with its own challenges and opportunities. The teams that take time to stretch, to regroup, and to recharge are the ones with enough energy left to play their best when the game is truly on the line. Your people aren't just in today's lineup. They're in for your season. Protect their energy, and you'll protect your ability to win.

29

Walk-Off Win – Closing Big Deals at the Last Moment

Delivering Under Pressure When Everything Is on the Line

Baseball Principle

In Game 7 of the 2001 World Series, the Arizona Diamondbacks faced the three-time defending champion New York Yankees. The stage was as big as it gets, tied in the bottom of the ninth, bases loaded, one out, and the game's most feared closer, Mariano Rivera, on the mound.

Luis González, a steady hitter but not known for overpowering swings, stepped into the box. On the second pitch, he didn't try to crush the ball. He simply stayed within himself, read the delivery, and dropped a soft bloop single over the drawn-in infield. The winning run scored. The Diamondbacks were World Series Champions, just four years after their expansion franchise was born.

It wasn't a towering home run or a moment built on brute strength. It was about composure, precision, and executing the right swing for the moment. González didn't get caught up in the pressure. He trusted his preparation and delivered exactly what his team needed. Walk-off wins like this remind us, that victory often comes not from trying to do everything, but from doing the right thing at exactly the right time.

Business Strategy

Walk-off wins in business are the moments when everything you have worked for comes down to a single opportunity. It might be the final presentation to a board of directors, the closing argument in a high-stakes negotiation, or the investor presentation that determines the future of your company. These are not routine innings. These are the bottom of the ninth, two outs, full-count moments where clarity, preparation, and presence decide everything.

These wins are rarely the result of improvisation. They belong to the teams who have rehearsed until their message is second nature, who enter the room with unity and calm, and who know how to translate complex work into one decisive, yet compelling story. They succeed because they understand that walk-off moments are not about showing everything you can do. They are about delivering the one message that matters most, at the exact time it matters most.

Every organization will face its walk-off moment. When it comes, the spotlight will not measure effort. It will measure execution. The teams who have built trust, sharpened their focus, and prepared for that moment are the ones who walk away with the win.

Real-World Example

A growing logistics firm was in the final running for a multimillion-dollar government contract. After months of proposals, site visits, and endless paperwork, the agency surprised the finalists with one last step. Teams were required to participate in an in-person interview with decision-makers from multiple departments. It was the bottom of the ninth. One more swing would decide everything.

Rather than defaulting to polished executives and recycled slide decks, the firm made a bold choice. They brought their operations lead and customer success manager, the very people who would manage the contract day-to-day. What the agency heard was not buzzwords or lofty promises, but practical expertise and real stories of how the team solved problems for other clients. The answers were grounded, confident, and authentic.

The meeting ended with one closing line that shifted the tone completely. What else would make you feel confident working with us? That single question opened a candid conversation, turning the session from a pitch into a partnership. Within weeks, the firm was formally awarded the contract through the procurement process.

It was their walk-off win, not because of a flashy presentation, but because they delivered the right message with the right people, at exactly the right moment.

Business Tip

To deliver in walk-off situations, apply these strategies:

- Know your audience's real concerns and craft a message that speaks to their challenges, not just your capabilities
- Lead with clarity by simplifying your value proposition so it lands even under pressure
- Rehearse real-world pressure scenarios by simulating high-stakes environments with your team
- Leave space for human connection and invite conversation, not just presentation

Walk-off wins are created long before the final swing. They come from teams that know how to finish.

Final Thought

A walk-off win is rarely about pure luck. It is about preparation meeting the right moment. It's about having the determination to execute when the stakes are highest. Luis González didn't try to overpower Mariano Rivera in Game 7 of the 2001 World Series, he stayed composed, read the situation, and delivered the exact swing the moment required.

Your walk-off moment may not come with cheering crowds, but it will arrive when the deadline is closing in, the stakes are high, and every decision hangs on your next move. When that moment comes, you will not have time to scramble or gather information. You will either be ready, or you will not.

Read the signs early and trust the analytics before the pressure hits. Anticipate the moments others miss. Build the relationships, systems, and confidence you'll rely on when the spotlight finds you. Because when you perform under pressure, you don't just meet a goal, but you shift momentum.

You change the story. You redefine what's possible for your team. Like a walk-off hit, that kind of win echoes long after the scoreboard resets.

30

Celebrate the Pennant – Recognizing Long-Term Success

Marking Milestones and Honoring the Journey

Baseball Principle

In 1995, the Cleveland Indians ended a 41-year drought by winning the American League pennant and returning to the World Series for the first time since 1954 under the leadership of general manager John Hart and manager Mike Hargrove. For a franchise and a fanbase that had endured decades of heartache with their last World Series Championship in 1948, long rebuilds, and losing seasons, this was not just a playoff run, it was a rebirth.

Led by stars like Albert Belle, Kenny Lofton, Manny Ramirez, and Jim Thome, the Indians were electric starting on Opening Day. They stormed through the regular season with speed, power, and precision, and when the postseason came, they delivered with both heart and hustle. Every game at Jacobs Field felt like a celebration with signs waving, drums pounding, the stadium shaking with noise and belief.

When the final out of the ALCS was recorded, Cleveland erupted. Fans embraced in the stands. Tears flowed. Generations who had only heard stories of the 1954 team were suddenly living their own euphoria they had once dreamed about. They had not won the World Series, but they had earned their place back on baseball's biggest stage. That alone was worth everything.

The proverbial pennant is more than a piece of fabric. It is a symbol of resilience, proof that the climb matters as much as the summit, and a reminder that sometimes the greatest victories are the ones that prove you belong.

Business Strategy

Long-term success often blurs together. One major project is barely complete before the next one demands attention. Teams work tirelessly for months, yet the milestones pass with little more than a quick email or a line in a report. Over time, this erodes meaning. The work feels endless. The purpose feels distant and unpersonal.

Great leaders understand that momentum does not just come from incremental achievement. It comes from recognition. Championship moments in business might be completing a five-year turnaround plan, delivering a once-in-a-generation infrastructure project, expanding into new markets, or rebuilding public trust after a crisis. These wins are not routine victories. They are the culmination of discipline, resilience, and countless daily sacrifices that often go unseen.

When leaders stop to acknowledge and celebrate these season-defining moments, they give the team more than a party. They give them ownership of the story. A celebration can remind employees of the obstacles they overcame, the relationships they built, and the difference their work made for others. That memory becomes fuel. The kind of pride and connection that carries them into the next season with renewed energy.

Celebration is not fluff. It is team building strategy. It is how great teams turn one chapter of success into a culture of sustained excellence.

Real-World Example

A large public school district had spent five years implementing a districtwide literacy initiative aimed at ensuring every third-grade student was reading at or above grade level. The effort spanned hundreds of classrooms, dozens of community partners, and countless hours of teacher training, curriculum refinement, and parental engagement.

When the final year's data confirmed record-breaking results, surpassing every state benchmark, the district didn't just release the numbers in a press statement. Instead, they held a "Reading Champions Day" at the local civic center. Students from each school were invited to read excerpts from their favorite books on stage. Teachers were recognized for their innovation and persistence. Community volunteers who had served as reading mentors received certificates and standing ovations.

Local media covered the celebration, capturing the joy of students and the pride of educators. The event didn't just honor an achieved goal, it reminded everyone of the years of dedication, collaboration, and belief that had made it possible. That shared moment of pride strengthened relationships, inspired new community partnerships, and built lasting momentum for the next phase of the district's educational vision.

Business Tip

To make celebration a meaningful part of your leadership strategy:

- Recognize the process, not just the outcome by honoring the late nights, hard choices, and resilience that made the win possible
- Tailor your recognition by making it personal, not performative
- Remind your team who they helped and why it matters
- Include partners, clients, and stakeholders in the celebration when appropriate
- Document the moment with photos, videos, and stories extend the life of the win and inspire future teams

Celebration is not a luxury. It is a leadership discipline that deepens culture and energizes performance.

Final Thought

When the 1995 Cleveland Indians clinched the American League pennant, the celebration was about more than winning a season. It was about reclaiming a story. It honored decades of struggle, the loyal fans who never stopped believing, and the team that brought hope back to a city hungry for a championship. The players weren't just raising a flag. They were lifting the weight of decades off the shoulders of an entire community. In fact, the city of Cleveland was so proud, they threw them a parade through the streets of downtown even though the Indians lost the World Series.

Your team has those stories too. The long projects that tested patience. The quarters that demanded grit. The people who showed up every single day, often without recognition, to keep the dream alive.

Do not wait for the ultimate victory to celebrate their work. Mark the moments when the tide turned, when the breakthrough happened, when the impossible became possible. Even if the final goal is still ahead, those milestones matter.

When you raise your own banner, whether it's closing a major deal, completing a complex rollout, or reaching a long-sought benchmark, you're doing more than recognizing an achievement. You're telling your team this achievement mattered, and that everyone on the team mattered. Team celebrations create a long-lasting legacy to commitment.

That feeling fuels the next climb. Success isn't defined by one finish line. It's built through every step, every lesson, and every moment you choose to keep going. It's in the championship flags you raise with the gratitude you carry for how far you've come. Because real success isn't just reaching the top. It's becoming the kind of leader who celebrates every milestone along the way to let your team know they matter, are valued, and appreciated.

🎬 Movie Break: *Major League* 🎬

Turning Underdogs into Contenders with Culture and Unity

Baseball Principle

Major League begins as a baseball team set up for failure. The new owner of the Cleveland Indians doesn't just expect the team to lose. She wants them to lose badly. She stacks the roster with unknowns, has-beens, and rookies in hopes of justifying a franchise move to another city. Theoretically on paper, the season is already over before it begins.

The players figure out the plan and realize they aren't supposed to succeed. For some teams, that would be the end with a slow, inevitable collapse. But not with these guys, as their team chose to fight back. Frustration became fuel. Skepticism became solidarity.

At the heart of the transformation is Jake Taylor, a veteran catcher whose knees are nearly shot but whose understanding of people is unmatched. He isn't the most talented player on the roster, but he's the one who keeps the clubhouse together. Jake knows when to push, when to listen, and when to set the example quietly by doing the hard work himself.

Around him, Rick "Wild Thing" Vaughn, Willie Mays Hayes, Pedro Cerrano, Roger Dorn, Eddie Harris, and other misfit teammates begin to evolve, not because they were ordered to, but because they chose to. They stop playing for individual stats and start playing for each other. Little moments, a shared joke or an unselfish play, become building blocks of trust.

What began as quiet sabotage turns into genuine synergy. The players own their season. The front office might control the roster, but the team now controls its story. That change from management to the people doing the work is what flips the season on its head.

Business Strategy

Every organization will face its *Major League* moment, the one where expectations are low, leadership is absent or unclear, and the path forward looks bleak. The temptation is to disengage, to go through the motions, to wait for someone else to fix things.

The film teaches a different lesson. Adversity can be the spark that brings a team together. The difference isn't always talent, it's trust. The shift isn't always structural, it's cultural.

Jake Taylor never campaigned for a title or demanded authority. He led by showing up, steadying the clubhouse, and creating a sense of purpose where it needed to be cultivated from within. He became the thermostat, not the thermometer by setting the tone instead of reacting to it.

There are culture creators in your organization. They're the project manager who checks in on the intern before a big presentation. The account executive who bridges departments when communication stalls. The operations lead who quietly solves problems without demanding credit.

When performance lags or leadership falters, teams don't just need orders, they need clarity. They need a rallying point. Teams are made of individuals and individuals need someone to believe in them first, so they can start believing in themselves.

Real-World Example

Consider companies that emerge from crisis with stronger identities. In startup environments or team restructures, resources are often thin, and vision may be unclear. Yet the most successful groups are built from within.

In its early years, Southwest Airlines faced a similar crossroad. Short on planes, understaffed, and battling larger competitors, it had every excuse to play defense. Instead, it rallied around a simple mission of getting customers from point A to point B with friendliness, humor, and efficiency.

The culture became a differentiator. Flight attendants sang safety instructions. Pilots greeted passengers at the gate. Employees treated each other like teammates, not just coworkers. These were not corporate mandates but were personal choices by people who believed in the mission.

The airline didn't just survive the crisis. It emerged with one of the strongest brand identities in the industry. Just like the Indians in *Major League*, Southwest's success was built from within, by people who decided to own the story instead of letting someone else write it.

Business Tip

To lead through a challenging environment and transform dysfunction into direction:

- Focus on shared goals that connect across job titles and personalities
- Empower informal leaders to carry the team culture from the inside out
- Reinforce unity through rituals, humor, and shared identity
- Encourage self-management from the bottom up, not just top-down mandates
- Let trust and clarity replace control and micromanagement

You do not need to fix everything at once. You need to show people what they are capable of by rallying together.

Final Thought

Major League may make you laugh, but its leadership truth can hit you right in the gut because we've all been there. We've all faced the season that felt lost before it started, the team that seemed thrown together, and the goal that felt out of reach with an inept boss.

The movie reminds us that underdogs don't win by accident. They win because someone refuses to let the circumstances define the outcome. They win because trust grows where doubt once lived, because belief is shared until it becomes unshakable.

Lead like Jake Taylor. Not because you're the flashiest, but because you're the one who will steady the room when everyone else is ready to give up. The one who will remind your team that what you build together, inside the clubhouse, the boardroom, or the breakroom, matters more than anything an owner, competitor, or critic can say.

One day, your team will look back on a project, a season, or a turnaround and realize it wasn't just a win, it was their win. They'll remember how it felt to believe again. They'll remember that you believed in them first.

That feeling endures long after the final out. In business, as in baseball, the greatest victories go far beyond the numbers. They live in the effort that no one saw, the trust built between teammates, and the pride of knowing you gave everything for something bigger than yourself. The wins that matter most aren't recorded on a stat sheet. They're remembered in the hearts of the people who made them possible.

⚾ Section 4: Precision ⚾

31

Communicate with Intention Using the Right Signals – Messaging Strategy

Effective Messaging Begins with Intentional Listening

Baseball Principle

The game within the game is often silent. Before PitchComm, the catcher's fingers would flick between his knees, signaling the next pitch. The third-base coach still swipes his arm or taps his chest, issuing game strategy to the runner. Even the batter will give a subtle signal to the dugout to acknowledge the plan. The most successful teams are the ones that master this coded language, which is intentional, responsive, and precise.

Few players embodied reading the signs better than David Eckstein. He lacked the imposing physical presence of many stars, but he became indispensable because he mastered the details others overlooked. Eckstein had a reputation for reading pitchers, studying opponents' tendencies, and responding to the smallest signs. He was not trying to outmuscle anyone. He was trying to out-think them by reading the signals he was given.

In the 2006 World Series, his ability to listen to what the game was telling him made all the difference. After struggling early, he locked into the Detroit Tigers' pitching patterns, picked up subtle tells, and changed his approach. The result was a breakout 4-for-5 performance with three doubles in Game 4, shifting the momentum of the series and earning him World Series MVP honors. He proved that success often comes not from brute force, but from careful observation of what the situation is telling and then delivering clear execution.

For Eckstein, signals were not background noise, they were the foundation of strategy. He turned awareness into action, communication into confidence, and intention into championships. His career was a masterclass in how listening and adjusting, even in subtle ways, can change the outcome of the game. In fact, he is the only starting shortstop in MLB history to win a World Series in both the American and National Leagues.

Business Strategy

The most effective leaders and communicators operate with the discipline of a veteran catcher reading the situation before calling the pitch. Leaders don't rush to fill silence with words or flood inboxes with noise. They listen before they speak. They read the room before they present. They assess audience needs before deciding what to say and when to say it. Every signal, verbal or nonverbal, formal or informal, provides cues about timing, tone, and trust.

Too often, messaging becomes reactive. A company fires off a quick email blast to employees without considering morale. A rushed social media post goes live without sensing the public mood.

A corporate statement gets published without context, sparking more questions than confidence. In each case, the result is not transparency but confusion.

Strategic communicators resist that impulse by reading all the internal and external signals. They pause. They take the temperature of the team. They weigh the stage of the project. They reflect on the emotional state of their audience and the internal dynamics of their team. Then they deliver words that carry not just information but a deeper meaning and purpose.

Great communication isn't about commanding all the attention in the room, making it all about you. It's about sending the right signals and delivering a message that's unmistakably clear. True communication leadership is intentional by knowing exactly why you're speaking, what you're signaling, and who you're trying to reach. Effective communication arrives with purpose, connects through empathy, and earns trust by demonstrating that you not only know what to say, but also when to stay silent.

Real-World Example

A family-owned florist shop was preparing to release a new sleek online ordering platform. Internally, the rollout was celebrated as a major modernization, faster transactions, digital payments, automated delivery tracking. But in early conversations with long-time customers, a different reality surfaced. Many of their most loyal patrons were older, less comfortable with technology, and deeply attached to the personal touch of phone orders and handwritten notes.

Instead of pushing ahead with only the digital message, the florist paused and reframed the rollout. They introduced in-store tutorials for using the website, kept a dedicated phone line for personal orders, and emphasized how the new system could complement, rather than replace, the personal service customers valued. The marketing campaign highlighted stories of customers using both options, showing flexibility rather than forcing change.

By listening and adjusting their approach, the florist avoided alienating their core base. Customers felt seen and supported, and the shop not only maintained loyalty but also gained new clients who appreciated both the tradition and the convenience. The upgrade succeeded because the communication was not just smart, it was sensitive to the customer base and garnered results.

Business Tip

To communicate with intention, leaders must train themselves and their teams to read the signs before acting:

- Collect feedback, observe patterns, and understand emotional context before crafting your message
- Identify what they need to hear in the moment, not just what you want to say
- Even the best message falls flat if the moment is wrong, so be strategic about when and how you communicate

- Establish consistency with what you say and what you do builds credibility and trust
- Remove jargon, focus your structure, and speak in terms that connect emotionally as well as logically

The strongest messages are rooted in empathy and based on listening. Signal your strength with simplicity.

Final Thought

A missed sign can flip the entire game with a runner stranded, an out wasted, and momentum lost. The smallest lapse of attention can cost everything. The stakes are just as high off the ballfield. A poorly timed message, a tone-deaf response, or a failure to read the room can damage credibility, weaken trust, and derail opportunity.

The leaders who excel are the ones who slow down enough to watch, to listen, and study before they act. They know when to nod, when to pause, and when to swing. Like a catcher adjusting the call after reading a batter's stance, or a coach signaling the perfect hit-and-run, they communicate with intention, not assumption.

Train yourself to see before you say with the right signals. Build the discipline to listen before you lead. When the moment comes, deliver with purpose so your signal cuts through the noise. Because in both baseball and business, wins aren't earned by those who talk the most, they're earned by those who are understood the best by connecting the dots.

32

Check the Coach – Clarity, Patience, & Team Alignment

Discipline and Trust When the Game is on

Baseball Principle

Even the most talented hitters do not step into the box expecting to swing at everything. They look down the line to the third base coach, waiting for the signal that sets the strategy. Swinging without that alignment is not just risky, as it can derail the entire inning. Sometimes, the most important instruction a batter can receive is silence. They must trust themselves with the confidence to deliver in the clutch.

That discipline is what defined hitters like Wade Boggs and Joe Mauer. Neither was known for raw power, but both earned reputations as some of the most disciplined hitters of their eras. Boggs could foul off pitch after pitch, refusing to chase outside the zone until the right pitch came. Mauer, with his patient eye and ability to read pitchers, built entire at-bats on restraint. He waited for the moment when the count, and the team's plan, worked in his favor to deliver.

These two Hall of Famers' greatness came not just from contact ability, but from trust in their approach, in their coaches, and in the strategy that shaped their game. They understood that a swing without purpose was worse than no swing at all. Their discipline sent a message. They were not just playing their game but also playing the team's game. In the biggest moments, that patience often became the difference between grounding out recklessly and delivering the hit that moved the team forward.

Business Strategy

Most teams don't stumble because they lack skill. They stumble because they lack alignment. One department chases its own metrics, while another pushes toward a different finish line. Individuals press ahead without knowing how their work connects to the larger mission. Theoretically on paper, everyone looks busy. The reality is the team is swinging without a signal and moving in many different directions.

The result is predictable with miscommunication, duplicated effort, wasted resources, and frustration that eventually turns into friction. What feels like progress is really motion without momentum. Teams cannot win heading in many different directions.

Strong organizations resist that urge to swing at everything. They slow down just long enough to check the coach to make sure the approach is clear, the signals are understood, and the players know their role in the inning ahead. That glance for direction is not softness, it is wisdom. It shows discipline, maturity, and trust.

When teams take the time to align, the swing that follows carries more weight. It connects with purpose. It drives results. It builds confidence when every player is part of the same plan. In the long run, that kind of alignment doesn't just win the at-bat, it wins the season.

Real-World Example

A nonprofit was preparing to launch its most ambitious fundraising campaign to date. Excitement was building across the organization. The creative team was finalizing ads and social media content. Field staff were already reaching out to community partners. Development officers were drafting appeals to major donors. On the surface, the nonprofit appeared ready to swing.

In the final alignment meeting, a regional director raised a concern that brought everyone to a stop. They asked if the organization was truly telling the same story. That simple question prompted a closer review, and the leadership team quickly discovered that two competing narratives were already in motion. One positioned the campaign as a push for immediate revenue. The other framed it as an effort to strengthen long-term donor relationships to further their core mission.

If the campaign had launched with that divide, supporters would have received conflicting messages. Donors would have been confused about the true purpose of the effort, and that confusion could have quickly eroded trust. Rather than pushing ahead, leadership chose to pause. They took the time to clarify the core purpose, unify the language, and ensure that every department spoke with one voice. They were checking for the signals.

The launch was delayed two months, but when it went live, the campaign was focused, intentional, and aligned. The results were historic with record-breaking donor engagement, stronger collaboration between departments, and a renewed sense of unity across the organization. That pause, that moment of stopping to check the coach, did not slow their success. It was the very reason they achieved it.

Business Tip

To ensure your team only moves when the signals are aligned:

- Define and repeat the big-picture goal before launching any major initiative
- Build in moments to pause and assess alignment before critical decisions
- Make it safe for team members to ask, are we clear on the goal
- Celebrate the teams who wait for clarity before charging ahead
- Sometimes the strongest move is not to act until direction is confirmed

A pause with purpose is often more valuable than action without logic.

Final Thought

One missed signal can change everything when every teammate is not aligned. A runner takes off too soon, a hitter swings at the wrong time, and what could have been a rally turns into a rally killer. Timing matters. Simplicity matters and trust in the signal to create team cohesion matters most of all.

The same truth applies back in the office. Charging ahead without alignment doesn't just waste effort, it erodes trust. Good intentions get lost in mixed messages, projects stall, and opportunities slip away. What feels like action can quickly become distractions with failing results.

The best teams know that speed alone doesn't win. Unity does. They trust the process, wait for clarity, and act only when the signal is clear to everyone. That discipline doesn't slow them down. It makes every swing count without the pressure to get the project out the door.

When the signal is unclear, the best leaders resist the urge to rush forward. Real leadership is not about being the brashest voice or the first to act. It is about having the courage to pause, the patience to align, and the wisdom to understand that lasting success is never about who moves first. It is about who has the discipline to move together, with clarity and purpose, when the moment is right.

33

Huddle on the Mound – Real-Time Corrections in Communication

Quick Pivots with a Trusted Voice Prevent Bigger Problems

Baseball Principle

In the 1986 National League Championship Series, the New York Mets were locked in a tense Game 6 against the Houston Astros. The season was in the balance. Pitcher Jesse Orosco struggling on the mound during the bottom of the 14th inning. The Mets team captain and first baseman Keith Hernandez took control of the situation.

He marched to the mound, not as the manager, but as the long-standing veteran on the team. Hernandez reminded Orosco of the bigger picture, cracked a joke to ease the tension, and settled his fellow infielders with the confidence of a veteran who had been there before. According to Hernandez, he said, "Jesse, if you throw another fastball we are going to fight."

That impromptu mound visit reset the tone. Orosco then struck out Kevin Bass with multiple sliders to end the game. The Mets won the game in the 16th inning, clinched the pennant, and advanced to the World Series to face the Boston Red Sox.

It was not a pitching change. It was not a confrontation. It was a leadership moment. One that showed how the right words, delivered at the right time, can steady a team under pressure and shift the outcome of a season.

Business Strategy

Too many teams push forward even when something feels off. The strategy is vague. Messages don't quite match. Team members sit in meetings confused but silent. Instead of stopping to address the gap, the default is often to keep going and hope it works itself out.

Great communicators and leaders understand the value of a well-timed mound visit. Just as a catcher or coach walks to the pitcher's mound to reset the moment, leaders step in to pause and realign. It might mean stopping mid-presentation to explain critical details, pulling the team together for a quick huddle when a project drifts, or asking the quietest voice in the room for input when tension is rising.

These small interventions prevent big problems. They show awareness and humility. More importantly, they signal to the team that accuracy, alignment, and clarity matter more than rushing to finish. A short pause today can save weeks of wasted effort tomorrow.

Real-World Example

A health care organization was midway through launching a multilingual awareness campaign when an internal report flagged a critical issue. The Spanish-language messaging, though technically accurate, came across as flat and disconnected from the cultural nuance of the Puerto Rican audience it was intended to reach.

Instead of waiting until the campaign concluded to address the problem, the project manager called an immediate cross-team huddle. Native-speaking Puerto Rican advisors were brought in, the tone and phrasing were updated, and the revised content was redistributed within a few weeks.

The impact was immediate. Local engagement across the intended Spanish-speaking audience nearly doubled. The win didn't come from getting everything perfect at the launch. It came from the team's willingness to pause, listen, and make the right adjustment in real time.

That quick mound visit didn't just save the campaign. It built trust with the audience. The change showed the organization's commitment to communication that is truly connected with their outcome.

Business Tip

To make course corrections when it matters most:

- Create a culture where real-time feedback is welcomed, not feared
- Watch confusion, frustration, or disengagement as signs to pause
- Good ideas and red flags can come from any level of the org chart
- A timely adjustment is better than a flawless fix too late
- Use follow-up time to capture lessons and strengthen future agility

Corrections do not signal failure. They show a commitment to excellence and to each member of the team.

Final Thought

When the pressure rises and the game feels like it could slip away, great leaders don't disappear into the dugout, they step forward with presence. In the 1986 NLCS, Keith Hernandez gave us that picture of leadership. He saw his pitcher unraveling, the energy of the inning tilting the wrong way. He didn't wait for the manager or hope things corrected themselves. He jogged to the mound, spoke a few calm words, and gave his team a moment to breathe. It wasn't a dramatic speech. It was composure in action, and it changed the inning.

Business has those same moments. A meeting veers off course. A project frays under deadline pressure. A client call turns tense. In those situations, silence isn't safety, it's surrender. The team looks for someone who will name the problem, reset the focus, and bring calm into chaos.

Your words in those moments carry more weight than you realize. They can steady the room, rebuild trust, and remind people of the plan. Leadership doesn't always come with a title or a script.

It comes with the courage to walk to the mound and the wisdom to say just enough to turn doubt into belief.

One day, your team will remember less about the metrics or the meeting agenda and more about how you showed up when the pressure was mounting. Step up. Speak with simplicity. Be calm in the storm. The right presence at the right time can be the difference between unraveling and rallying your team to victory.

34

Signal from the Dugout – Internal Messaging Frameworks

Lead from Within with Consistent Communication That Drives Alignment

Baseball Principle

The dugout is more than a bench and place for the players and coaches to sit during a game. The dugout is the command center. The manager and coaches see the whole field, spot patterns, and decide when to act. A sign to lay down a bunt, to steal a base, or a call for a pitchout isn't just about communicating tactical advantages, it's about trust. It tells the players to stick to the plan because the entire team is pulling in the same direction.

One of the clearest demonstrations of dugout leadership came during the 2023 World Baseball Classic, when Team Japan captured the title against some of the most talented rosters in the world. Japan wasn't the biggest or flashiest team, but they were the most coordinated. Every signal mattered, every shift had purpose, and every player trusted the system.

Manager Hideki Kuriyama and his staff emphasized precision, communication, and shared responsibility. From sacrifice bunts to perfectly timed pitching changes, Japan executed strategies that only worked because everyone in the dugout believed in them. The players didn't guess, they trusted the call.

That trust created momentum. When Shohei Ohtani struck out Mike Trout to end the championship game, it wasn't just a personal duel between two superstars and teammates, it was the culmination of a team that had mastered communication and cohesion at every level. Team Japan didn't win because they had the most power. They won because they had a framework of communication and trust that aligned every player, every pitch, and every decision toward one goal.

Business Strategy

The boardroom is like the dugout, and your internal signals are your messaging framework. Yet many organizations put all their energy into external communication, crafting campaigns for customers, talking points for media, and presentation decks for investors. Too often forgetting that their most important audience is sitting inside their own walls.

When employees don't know the strategy, don't understand what's behind decisions, or don't hear consistent expectations from leadership, what you get is confusion instead of coordination. Silos and individualism replace teamwork. Guesswork replaces execution.

A strong internal messaging framework works like dugout signals. It doesn't just push information down. It creates alignment across the organization. It tells people what we are going to accomplish together. It shares with everyone why it matters and each individual fits into the plan.

When a company launches a new initiative, navigates change, or faces a crisis, the simplicity of its internal signals determines whether employees act with confidence, or hesitate in doubt. The best leaders know their external voice will never be stronger than their internal alignment.

Real-World Example

A law firm was preparing to introduce a new case management platform across all its offices. Externally, the rollout looked polished, updated branding, a client-facing portal, along with a client newsletter and a press release promising efficiency and innovation. Inside the firm, the signals weren't clear. Attorneys were unsure how the platform would change their daily workflow. Paralegals worried about losing access to familiar tools. Office managers were left to interpret the transition on their own.

Recognizing the disconnect, firm leadership called timeout and reassessed the situation. They launched a weekly internal brief that went beyond technical updates. Each message included FAQs (frequently asked questions), sample client responses, and spotlight stories from early adopters who were already benefiting from the system. Practice group leaders were trained to serve as early adopters by reinforcing consistent language, expectations, and support in their own teams.

The change in results was immediate. Staff began to feel informed instead of being left out. Confidence in the platform grew, adoption accelerated, and client service improved. The external rollout succeeded not because of sleek marketing, but because the firm finally aligned its internal communication.

Business Tip

To build a strong dugout structure with an internal messaging framework that aligns the team:

- Use regular internal updates (emails, huddles, videos) that become part of your team's coordination
- Train and empower managers to reinforce key messages in their own voice
- Eliminate unnecessary jargon and create consistent terminology across teams
- Connect updates to values, vision, and purpose so people know why it matters
- Invite questions, feedback, and field-level input so communication flows both ways

When your internal messages are strong, your team acts in sync. Not out of obligation, but out of belief.

Final Thought

Great teams don't stumble their way through high-stakes moments. They don't rely on guesswork or hope. They execute a shared plan. In baseball, that clarity often comes from the dugout. One signal from a manager, delivered at exactly the right time, tells the team we've got this. Trust the plan and now go execute.

Your internal communication in your business works the same way. Before your organization faces the public, before the big presentation, the campaign launch, or the client meeting, your own dugout must be aligned. Your people need to know not just what to do, but why it matters, and how they fit into the bigger picture.

When you give that reassurance, something powerful happens. Teams don't just comply, they commit. They move with confidence, speak with one voice, and deliver with conviction.

That is the difference between groups that react and teams that win. The signal doesn't have to be loud, but it must be clear. When your signals are transparent, your people won't just follow instructions, they'll believe in the mission and fight to succeed.

35

Talk to the Catcher – Feedback Loops & Peer Transparency

Great Teams Communicate with Courage and Consistency

Baseball Principle

Few relationships on the field are as critical as the one between pitcher and catcher. The catcher is the strategist, the communicator, and often the steady presence when the game feels like it could tip at any moment. No one embodied that role better than Hall of Fame catcher Johnny Bench, the backbone of the Cincinnati Reds' Big Red Machine in the 1970s winning multiple World Series.

Bench wasn't just calling individual pitches, instead he was strategically calling the game. His ability to read hitters, anticipate situations, and guide pitchers through pressure moments set him apart. Teammates often said that throwing to Bench behind the plate gave them confidence, because they knew he wasn't simply catching the ball, he was thinking two steps ahead.

When a pitcher struggled, Bench didn't hesitate to jog out to the mound. He didn't go out to lecture. He went out to connect. Sometimes it was a quick adjustment. Sometimes it was just a reminder to breathe. Whatever the message, it was delivered with clarity, trust, and presence.

That is why Bench is remembered not only for his power at the plate, but for his leadership behind it. He turned feedback into trust, and trust into championships. For the Reds, talking to the catcher didn't just improve performance, it defined their dynasty.

Business Strategy

Teams often push forward without stopping to check in. Feedback becomes an annual formality or an afterthought once a project is over. Just as a catcher walks to the mound to steady a pitcher, real-time communication between colleagues, especially peer-to-peer, is what keeps a team focused and confident under pressure.

Great teams don't wait for performance reviews or exit interviews to speak honestly. They build honest dialogue where feedback is candid, constructive, and expected. In practice, talking to the catcher in your organization might look like asking a teammate, what am I missing? Even saying, here's something I noticed that might help. Or how are you feeling?

These conversations aren't about hierarchy or authority, they're about alignment, trust, and shared success. When feedback is offered in the moment, with respect and clarity, it doesn't create friction. It creates fuel. It turns good performers into great ones, and great teams into champions.

Real-World Example

At a consulting firm, a client account team began slipping behind schedule after a key staff member unexpectedly had to deal with a family emergency in another state. Tension was rising, but instead of waiting for senior leadership to intervene, a catcher on the team decided to walk to the mound for a visit. Inviting the team for coffee, they spent twenty minutes being candid with each other, lying out where communication had broken down, where expectations were unclear, and how the workload could be adjusted between them.

That small, honest check-in changed the trajectory of the project. By realigning in real time, they avoided further delays, met their deadlines, and lifted morale across the team.

The turnaround didn't come from a grand strategy session or a top-down directive. It came because teammates created space to talk, listen, and steady each other in the moment. Just like a catcher jogging to the mound, that peer-to-peer conversation wasn't about hierarchy, it was about trust. Trust was the element that put the project back on track.

Business Tip

To build a culture where feedback feels like support, not judgment, use these practices:

- Encourage informal, timely conversations between teammates
- Leaders and peers alike should ask for input, not just give it
- Teach teams how to give and receive honest input with care and clarity
- Keep feedback action-oriented, not personal
- Follow up to show that feedback is valued and acted on

Feedback is not a confrontation. It is a collaboration surrounded with trust.

Final Thought

When Johnny Bench crouched behind the plate for the Cincinnati Reds, he was more than a catcher, he was a leader. His teammates trusted that if the game started to get away, he would be the first to notice, the first to steady them, and the first to remind them they weren't alone on the mound. Sometimes it was strategy, sometimes it was encouragement, but it was always a connection. That kind of trust was the heartbeat of the Big Red Machine, and it was one of the reasons they became back-to-back World Series champions.

In your organization, you'll face an inning when things get a little off the rails. The project that drifts, the client conversation that turns tense, the deadline that suddenly feels like too much. The easy mistake is to keep throwing pitches without stopping to check in. The best teams know better. They call time. They talk. They listen.

Don't be afraid to walk to the mound and discuss the situation. Ask the question. Listen to the honest answer. When teammates trust each other enough to speak the truth, even under stress, they do more than get through the inning. They build the kind of trust that wins the game, and they win together.

36

Mic Up Your MVPs – Employee Thought Leadership

Your Best Voices Deserve a Platform, So Let Them Lead the Conversation

Baseball Principle

No baseball team has embraced the power of "mic'd up" moments quite like the Savannah Bananas. More than just a barnstorming ball club, they've become a phenomenon by blending entertainment with authentic connection with their microphones in hand. Their players don't just perform on the field, they engage directly with fans, sharing personality, humor, and insight in real time.

Take Jackson Olson, the charismatic infielder whose energy, authenticity, and social media reach have made him one of the Bananas' biggest stars. Whether he's explaining his mid-game approach, joking with fans between innings, or hyping his teammates, Olson shows that leadership is not only about skill, but also about presence and connection.

Another player is Kyle "KJ" Jackson, whose creativity and confidence have turned him into both a star performer and a leader. When the camera is on him, KJ doesn't just entertain, he models enthusiasm, resilience, and joy. His voice amplifies the team's culture and reminds everyone that the Bananas' success is about how they make people feel.

By giving their stars a platform, the Bananas prove that when you hand the mic to your best voices. You don't just showcase talent, you build trust, loyalty, and leadership that extends far beyond the field. The team is not afraid to hand someone the microphone.

Business Strategy

In the workplace, your MVPs, the steady performers who deliver results, mentors peers, and build trust day after day, often shine quietly. Their impact is felt inside the organization but rarely amplified outside of it. Too often, their voices stay confined to team meetings or internal emails, when they could be shaping industry conversations.

Giving your MVPs a microphone means putting them in positions where their authenticity becomes your brand's credibility. That could mean giving them space to post insights on LinkedIn, letting them lead a webinar, sending them to present at an industry conference, or inviting them to brief clients directly. When employees with earned respect speak from experience, the message carries more weight than any press release or ad campaign.

People trust people more than they trust brands. When those people are your own culture carriers and trusted internal leaders, their voices don't just represent your company, they humanize it.

Real-World Example

An engineering pipeline infrastructure firm was preparing for a major industry conference. Traditionally, the spotlight would go to executives or senior directors. This time, the firm chose to feature a mid-career engineer who had led several data-driven projects with measurable community impact.

At first, they were nervous having never spoken on a national stage before. Their technical expertise was deep, their results were proven, and their story was real. When they shared practical examples of how their team had reduced waste, increased operational efficiency and improved safety. Their authenticity cut through the usual engineering jargon.

The response was overwhelming. Conference attendees lined up afterward to ask questions. A national trade publication highlighted their remarks. New clients reached out to the firm. Back home, staff across all levels of the organization said they felt proud seeing one of their own elevated as an industry voice.

The company gained visibility. They gained confidence and the industry gained a fresh, credible perspective. By giving the microphone to their MVP, the firm didn't just showcase a project, they showcased a leader, and in doing so, strengthened both their brand and their culture.

Business Tip

To cultivate and amplify employee thought leadership:

- Look beyond title and tenure and find the people who live your values and elevate others
- Encourage guest blog posts, podcast appearances, conference panels, or social media features
- Provide media training, writing help, or coaching so they feel prepared and confident
- Authenticity matters more than polish and let their real experience guide the message
- Align their personal insights with your organizational purpose to drive impact and coherence

When you let your best people speak, your brand voice becomes more human, more powerful, and more trusted.

Final Thought

The Savannah Bananas didn't become a sensation because they play the cleanest and most fundamentally sound brand of baseball. They became unforgettable through the energy of their players and the vision of their leader, Jesse Cole, whose signature yellow tuxedo, invites every fan into the experience. The Bananas let us hear the jokes, feel the energy, and connect with the personalities behind the game. Cole's goal isn't just to sell tickets. It's to create fans by turning baseball into something bigger than the scoreboard. Entertainment that is personal, emotional, and shared.

In your organization, the same opportunity exists. Your MVPs carry insights, creativity, and heart that deserve to be heard, not hidden. When an organization mic's them up, they don't just showcase skill, they showcase soul. You let people see not just what your company does, but why it matters through the voices they trust most.

Do not underestimate the power of letting your best people speak. Give them a platform. Give them the microphone. Let them lead conversations that carry your culture and your mission beyond the walls of your workplace.

When your people speak with authenticity, they do more than represent your organization and they invite others to believe in it. Belief is what builds fans, builds loyalty, and builds legacies that last.

37

Protect the Signs – Confidentiality & Internal Trust

Guarding What Matters Behind the Scenes

Baseball Principle

In today's game, pitchers and catchers often rely on the electronic PitchComm system to call pitches, a safeguard born from decades of sign stealing, baseball's oldest cat-and-mouse tradition. For generations, teams have tried to crack the opposing catcher's code from second base, hoping to predict the next pitch. Observational sign stealing has always walked a fine line between strategy and ethics, but when technology entered the mix, that line was crossed. The 2017 Houston Astros video sign stealing scandal proved how far things could go, shaking the very foundation of trust that holds the game together.

Yet beyond the headlines lies a deeper truth as signs exist because faith exists. When a catcher calls for a curveball, they're signaling belief. They're trusting that the pitcher will read, respond, and protect that shared code. Every sign is a quiet conversation built on faith, discipline, and confidentiality.

The moment those signals are exposed, the communication damage runs deeper than lost strategy. It erodes connection, unity, and belief in one another. In baseball, as in leadership, the team's strength isn't just in the plays they make. It's in the trust they protect when no one else is watching.

Business Strategy

Every organization runs on signals that are not meant for public view. Strategic plans, sensitive client data, private conversations, and candid feedback can shape decisions. How those signals are handled says more about culture than any mission statement on a wall.

When employees feel their input will be leaked, mocked, or dismissed, they stop sharing. When client information is treated carelessly, relationships erode. When leaders reveal sensitive discussions too soon, trust fractures. These are not just operational missteps. They are cultural wounds. Once trust is broken, morale sinks, collaboration slows, and reputations suffer in ways that are hard to repair.

Protecting confidentiality is not about secrecy. It is about respect. It is about proving to employees that their concerns matter, to clients that their information is safe, and to partners that discretion is part of their integrity. A team that knows the signals are protected feels free to innovate, to speak honestly, and to commit fully because they know what they share in confidence will be safeguarded.

The organizations that thrive are the ones that treat confidentiality as more than compliance. They treat it as the cornerstone of trust.

Real-World Example

A tech firm operating in stealth mode was preparing to launch a groundbreaking artificial intelligence platform that promised to reshape how its clients operated. The details, timeline, features, and pricing were tightly held by a small internal group. During a virtual networking event, one team member casually mentioned the upcoming release at an industry conference. Within hours, a competitor teased a suspiciously similar product on social media.

The leak was a wake-up call. The company realized the issue wasn't just about one careless comment, it was about culture. Employees didn't fully understand the importance of information discipline, nor did they feel connected enough to recognize how their words carried weight.

In response, leadership put new measures in place. This was accomplished with role-based access to sensitive information, clearer internal communication protocols, and updated onboarding that emphasized not just legal confidentiality, but cultural trust. The message was clear, protecting information wasn't a task for a few, it was a shared responsibility for all.

That moment of failure became a turning point. By reframing confidentiality as respect for one another and for the mission, the company rebuilt trust internally and strengthened its reputation externally.

Business Tip

To build and maintain internal trust around confidentiality:

- Define what is confidential, why it matters, and how to protect it
- Executives and managers must always model discretion and professionalism
- Strategically sharing sensitive data on a need-to-know basis, without fostering silos
- Reinforce policies during onboarding, and refresh regularly with real-world examples
- When people feel trusted and respected, they are more likely to protect what matters

Confidentiality is not just a policy. It is a signal that the team has each other's back.

Final Thought

Teams must trust the honest integrity of a sign. A quick look in the dugout or a subtle gesture from the catcher can strengthen the backbone of team commitment. They are trust in motion. Every player on the field relies on the certainty that the signal will be honored. When that trust breaks, when a sign is stolen, missed, or betrayed, the consequences ripple. Games are lost. Reputations tarnish. Entire seasons can be clouded by doubt.

Business works the same way. A whisper in the wrong room, an email forwarded too soon, or a strategy leaked carelessly can unravel months, even years, of hard work. Just like on the diamond, the cost is bigger than a single play. It erodes confidence, fractures relationships, and stalls momentum.

The best leaders understand that protecting information isn't about secrecy, it's about respect. It's about proving to your people that what is said in confidence stays in confidence. When teams know their conversations are safe, they speak with candor, share their best ideas, and take risks that lead to breakthroughs.

Trust is not built on stage, under bright lights, or in a press release. It is built behind the scenes, one sign, one conversation, one promise kept at a time. When that trust is strong, your team won't just play harder. They'll play together. Together is how you win.

38

The Change Up – Adapting Messaging on the Fly

Agile Communication in Real Time Under Real Pressure

Baseball Principle

Taking the concept a step further from our last chapter, even the best game plan can collapse if opponents begin to anticipate your moves. Pitchers and catchers know this, which is why they constantly guard against predictability with a quick change of signals. When a runner at second base starts signaling to the batter, when patterns become too obvious, or when the momentum feels like it is shifting, the catcher doesn't just hope for the best. They act.

During Game 6 of the 2016 NLCS, with a trip to the World Series on the brink, Cubs catcher Willson Contreras found himself facing that problem. The Dodgers' runners were starting to pick up the signs. Contreras noticed subtle shifts in the Dodgers' at-bats as swings were more targeted, players were more disciplined, and certain pitches weren't surprising them anymore. It wasn't luck because they were anticipating the pitch sequences.

Contreras didn't ignore it. He called time, jogged to the mound, and immediately changed the sign system with pitcher Kyle Hendricks. Instead of a simple one-sign pattern, they adopted a multi-sign, multi-location sequence that shifted with every batter and every base runner. The adjustment wasn't flashy. It was quiet, quick, and strategic, the kind of decision that only happens when leaders stay alert and respond in real time.

The impact was immediate. Hendricks locked in, Dodgers hitters became tentative, and the rhythm of the game shifted in Chicago's favor. Hendricks went on to deliver one of the most dominant starts of his career. Contreras showed what agile communication looks like in the biggest moments. You don't wait for the problem to grow. In leadership you own it, you adapt, and address the problem.

Business Strategy

For leaders, the parallel is obvious. You may prepare your message, your campaign, or your presentation with care, but once it is in the public arena, conditions can shift instantly. Competitors adjust. Audiences react. Headlines rewrite the context in real time. Just like a catcher protecting the strike zone, leaders must be ready to change the signals, adjust the tone, or reframe the story without losing their larger purpose.

Every organization values planning. Strategies, messaging frameworks, and talking points create confidence and clarity. When the circumstances shift, a competitor beats you to market, public sentiment changes overnight, or a crisis dominates the headlines, rigidity turns from strength to weakness.

In those moments, the best leaders don't cling to the script. They pivot with purpose. Adjusting tone, reworking messaging in real time, or rewriting internal talking points after an unexpected policy change doesn't signal weakness, it signals maturity.

Agility in communication isn't improvisation for its own sake. It's knowing your mission so well that you can flex your words without losing your anchor. It's the difference between scrambling to react and skillfully steering the message. Teams that can change without hesitation prove they aren't just prepared for perfect conditions, but they're prepared for reality.

Real-World Example

A retail chain was preparing to launch its highly anticipated holiday campaign. The theme was playful, lighthearted, and focused on family traditions. The ads were finalized, store displays were set, and press interviews were booked.

Then, just days before the launch, a devastating natural disaster struck one of the regions where the company had a large presence. Communities were grieving and families were displaced. Rolling out cheerful, upbeat messaging would have seemed tone-deaf and disconnected from reality.

Instead of forcing the original plan, the marketing team pivoted. They delayed certain ads, reframed messaging around community resilience, and committed resources to support local recovery efforts. Store managers were given talking points that emphasized compassion and care, not just sales.

The pivot worked. Customers praised the company's sensitivity. Media outlets highlighted the store's relief contributions. When the campaign rolled out as originally planned weeks later, it carried greater authenticity and connection, because the company showed it was willing to change the signs after the game had started.

Business Tip

To build the skill of responsive messaging:

- Watch news cycles, social sentiment, and emerging signals from your audience
- Know what you stand for, so your pivot keeps you rooted
- Train spokespeople and managers to adjust tone without waiting for top-down direction
- Practice "what if" scenarios to improve your ability to pivot under pressure
- After the pivot, reflect on what worked and why and build learning into the system

The game may change in real time. So must your message.

Final Thought

Changing the signs is not an act of panic, it is an act of leadership. When the other team begins to catch on, when the game shifts, when the pitcher looks in for guidance and the dugout responds with something new, it is a reminder that flexibility is as important as preparation. The best managers do not just use the original game plan. They adjust it because they understand the game is alive and always changing.

The same principle holds true every day in the workforce. The marketplace is not static. Neither are people, technology, or culture. What worked last quarter may feel out of touch today. A message that sounded bold yesterday might ring hollow after new events. Leaders who insist on sticking to the original script risk not only missing the moment but also losing the trust of their team, their partners, and their customers.

Adaptability does not mean abandoning the mission. It means knowing it so clearly that you can shift the words, the tone, or the tactics without ever losing sight of the vision. It means having the courage to acknowledge that circumstances have changed by being humble to recalibrate before small cracks become lasting fractures.

Great leaders read the field and communicate effectively. They sense when the environment shifts, they stay attuned to the mood of their people, and they adjust their voice so that it connects with authenticity and purpose. That kind of agility is not weakness, it is wisdom.

When you feel the signals no longer fit, do not be afraid to change them. Reframe the message. Reset the rhythm. Give your team a signal that reflects both the reality of the moment and the strength of your shared purpose. Leadership is not measured by how faithfully you deliver a rehearsed line but is measured by how skillfully you pivot without losing the trust of those who are counting on you.

39

Standing Tall on the Mound – Courage When the World Is Watching

Resilience, Presence, and the Power of Public Adversity

Baseball Principle

Jim Abbott's story is one of the most powerful in baseball history. Born without a right hand, Abbott faced doubt at every stage of his life. His family wondered if he could ever play sports. Scouts questioned if he could compete. Critics predicted that, at best, he might survive on the fringes of the game. Abbott proved them all wrong.

Not only did he pitch in the major leagues for a decade, but he did also it with grace, grit, and effectiveness. On September 4, 1993, he delivered a masterpiece. A no-hitter for the New York Yankees against the Cleveland Indians in the Bronx. The moment wasn't just about 27 outs and zero hits. It was about the courage to stand in the middle of Yankee Stadium, under the glare of the spotlight, and show the world that adversity does not define destiny.

Abbott wasn't simply pitching for himself. Every time he took the mound, he represented every child who had been told they couldn't, every person who had been overlooked, and every individual fighting to turn their limitation into strength. His presence on that stage was leadership in its purest form. He showed us that even when the world is measuring every move, you can inspire by staying composed, staying authentic, and standing tall.

Business Strategy

Leaders face their own Jim Abbott type moments every day. The pressure may not come from 50,000 fans in a stadium, but it comes from the decisions that shape people's lives. Leaders decide who gets an opportunity, who is trusted with responsibility, and who is invited to step onto the field. For some employees, the challenge is not talent or drive but being seen through the lens of their disability rather than their potential.

Great leaders know that these moments are not tests of an employee's limits, but of the leader's vision. When you give someone the chance to contribute, regardless of physical or intellectual challenges, you are not lowering expectations. You are raising belief. You are saying that what matters most is courage, effort, and the ability to grow.

Just as Abbott proved that a missing hand could not keep him from throwing a no-hitter in the major leagues, employees with obstacles to overcome often bring creativity and resilience that elevate the entire team. Leadership is about creating space for them to show it.

Real-World Example

A manager welcomed a new hire with a cognitive disability into the operations team they met volunteering with Special Olympics. Some colleagues were skeptical, assuming the new hire would struggle with detail-oriented tasks. Instead of sidelining them, the manager gave their new hire clear training, structured support, and the freedom to approach the work in their own way.

Within months, the new team member had become one of the most consistent and accurate contributors on the floor. Their focus, persistence, and positivity raised morale, and their presence reminded others that excellence is not defined by labels. The manager later admitted that the decision to give them a chance was one of the most rewarding leadership choices of their career.

Adversity did not limit this employee, but it revealed their strength. The leader who believed in them didn't just change a résumé, but they forever changed a life.

Business Tip

Create opportunities that focus on ability, not limitation.

- Seeing potential first, give employees with challenges meaningful roles, not token tasks.
- Provide the right support systems with clear expectations, accessible tools, and structured coaching.
- Celebrate effort and progress, not just perfection.
- Recognize that resilience, creativity, and grit often emerge strongest among those who have had to overcome obstacles.
- Remember that when you believe in someone before the world does, you don't just unlock their performance, but you unlock their loyalty and transform your culture.

Final Thought

Jim Abbott's no-hitter was more than a baseball achievement. It is etched into history not simply because he kept a lineup hitless, but because of what it symbolized. It was a triumph of resilience over doubt, of composure over criticism, of courage over every limitation the world tried to impose.

He showed that greatness is not measured only in talent or statistics, but in the ability to rise when everything says you should fall. It was proof that courage, resilience, and opportunity can rewrite every expectation. He showed the world that a limitation does not define a life, what defines it is the chance to stand on the mound and prove what is possible.

Your greatest legacy may not come from the projects you complete or the numbers you report. It may come from the people you choose to believe in when others hesitate. Every time you give someone the chance to step up, whether they are facing a physical disability, an intellectual challenge, or the quiet doubt of being underestimated, you create the possibility of transformation.

Adversity does not diminish potential. It amplifies potential when met with belief. As a leader, you hold the power to open that door. When you do, you are not just shaping a career. You are shaping a story of resilience that will echo far beyond your organization. Abbott reminds us that greatness is not about what you are given. It is about what you rise to do when someone believes in you enough to hand you the ball.

40

Team Chatter – Informal Culture & Communication Rhythm

How Everyday Interactions Shape Trust and Team Cohesion

Baseball Principle

In 1990, the Cincinnati Reds shocked the baseball world by sweeping the heavily favored Oakland Athletics in the World Series. On paper, the Reds weren't supposed to dominate. They didn't have the biggest stars or the largest payroll. What they had was chemistry and teamwork that kept them connected, focused, and confident while facing long odds.

One of the anchors of that championship run was Hall of Famer and that season's MVP, Barry Larkin. Larkin wasn't just a shortstop, he was the steady voice in the middle of the diamond, orchestrating the flow of the game in ways box scores could never capture. Pitch after pitch, he was talking, not for show, but for gamesmanship with simple leadership. He reminded his infielders of the number of outs. He directed where the ball should go if it came their way. When a teammate booted a grounder, Larkin was the first to shout encouragement, snapping them back into focus. When someone made the routine play, he celebrated it like it mattered, because to him, every play mattered.

That chatter became the heartbeat of the team. It wasn't random noise. It was structure, energy, and reassurance layered into every inning. Younger players leaned on it for confidence. Pitchers trusted it as a calming force behind them. Outfielders mirrored it to stay sharp and engaged. Larkin's leadership voice created a safety net, a constant reminder that no one was out there alone.

The Reds thrived not just because of raw talent, but because they refused to play silent baseball. From the dugout to the outfield, communication pulsed through the team, steady, consistent, and supportive. That talk-it-up-culture built trust, sharpened awareness, and kept everyone locked in from the first pitch to the final out. It was leadership not through speeches or titles, but through presence, words, and the discipline of never letting the game go quiet.

Business Strategy

Culture isn't built only in staff meetings or official strategy sessions. It's built in the small, everyday moments of connection with the hallway conversations, the quick check-ins before a presentation, a quick email message that says, I've got your back.

Just like the Reds in 1990, successful teams know that internal chatter is more than background noise, it creates trust. Informal communication keeps people aligned, sharp, and connected, even when they're spread across roles, locations, or projects.

Think of a project team under deadline pressure. When they're silent, tension grows, assumptions multiply, and mistakes creep in. The team needs to be talking, celebrating progress, reminding each other of key tasks, and calling out small wins as they build momentum. They stay in the game pitch by pitch, not just in the big milestones.

The best leaders don't just encourage communication when something goes wrong, they normalize it when things are going right. They understand that the chatter itself is part of performance. It's how teams learn to anticipate each other's moves, recover quickly from errors, and stay connected when the stakes rise.

In business, as in baseball, silence is rarely neutral. It often signals disconnect. Teams that keep the conversation flow consistently, authentically, and informally, build the trust and cohesion needed to face challenges together and win as one.

Real-World Example

A landscaping company managed dozens of crews across neighborhoods and commercial sites. The work was demanding with tight schedules, changing weather, and detailed client expectations. Early on, leadership noticed something simple but powerful. The most reliable crews weren't just the ones with the best tools or the most experienced. They were the ones that talked the most while they worked.

On one site, a foreman made it a habit to keep communication flowing. Quick reminders like, check the edging, great work on that cut, and even a well-timed joke. Crew members responded with updates, encouragement, and suggestions of their own. The chatter wasn't scripted. It was steady, supportive, and specific that created a cohesive team.

Over time, this professional banter created trust. Newer employees felt included and learned faster. Mistakes were caught before they became problems. Even on long, hot summer days, the crew stayed focused and connected. Clients noticed the difference. Jobs ran smoother, quality improved, and referrals increased.

The lesson was clear because success wasn't only in planning documents or the equipment trucks. It was in the drum beat of constant, informal communication that kept the team sharp and united. Just like on the ballfield, the chatter in the field became the culture that sustained the win.

Business Tip

To build and sustain a healthy dialogue of informal communication:

- Create space for non-task-oriented interactions
- Leaders should drop into casual chats or group threads
- Normalizing recognition beyond official awards
- Silence may signal disengagement or discomfort
- Joy is a powerful connector, even at work

Culture is not built in boardrooms. It is built in banter in everyday interactions.

Final Thought

A silent field is rarely a good sign. The 1990 Cincinnati Reds didn't dominate the World Series on raw skill alone over a physically stronger team with Mark McGwire and Jose Canseco. They won because they played together as a team and never stopped talking. Barry Larkin, their MVP and anchor at shortstop, kept his teammates connected with steady communication that carried through every inning. His voice by calling out plays, reinforced awareness and lifted teammates after mistakes. It built confidence. That constant dialogue turned a roster of talent into a unified team that played alert, focused, and together from the first pitch to the final out.

The same truth holds in any work team. An organization that talks consistently, checking in, sharing feedback, celebrating small wins, stays sharper and stronger than a team that only speaks up when something breaks. Just like the landscaping crew that built success through steady on-site chatter, your organization's culture is shaped less by what's written in memos and more by what's spoken in everyday moments.

Do not underestimate the power of informal communication. It turns isolation into inclusion, hesitation into action, and individuals into teammates. Encourage the chatter. Model it. Protect it. When people talk it up with purpose, they don't just get through the workday, they build the kind of trust and cohesion that wins championships.

🎬 Movie Break: *The Sandlot* 🎬

Transforming Potential into Confidence Through Trust

Baseball Principle

"You're killing me, Smalls." It is the movie's classic line we all remember, but the true magic of *The Sandlot* is not in the humor. It is in the heart. This is not a story about perfect baseball mechanics or polished players chasing championships. It is a story about a kid who just wants to belong.

Scotty Smalls moves to a new city showing up with no glove worth using, no idea how to throw, and no knowledge of the game's simplest rules. He is awkward, unsure, and clearly out of place. He is also willing to try, and in that willingness, something extraordinary happens.

Enter Benny "The Jet" Rodriguez, clearly the most talented player on the field, but more importantly, the group's quiet leader. Benny does not dismiss Smalls for his inexperience. He does not roll his eyes or leave him behind. Instead, he takes Smalls under his wing. He mentors with patience, he demonstrates kindness, and he creates space for Smalls to grow into something bigger than he ever imagined.

That is how great teams are built. Not by stacking rosters with the most natural talent, but by building a culture where growth is possible, where inclusion is prioritized, and where effort is valued as much as ability. *The Sandlot* is not comprised of the best players. It is about the best teammates.

Business Strategy

Every workplace has its version of Smalls. Someone new, someone untested, someone who does not yet know the game. They may not shine on day one. They may ask basic questions. They may struggle with confidence. Like Scotty Smalls, their greatest asset is their willingness to learn.

Benny shows us what leadership looks like in these moments. He does not just tell Smalls what to do. He models it. He invests in him. Most importantly, he makes Smalls feel like he belongs before he has proven anything on the field. That belief becomes the fuel for transformation.

Too often, businesses chase fully polished professionals, looking for the perfect hire instead of cultivating the talent already in the dugout. Résumés and credentials tell only part of the story. The rest depends on what happens when leaders invest, mentor, and create an environment where people can fail forward.

Organizations that embrace this mindset do not just fill roles, they build loyalty. They develop future leaders by creating cultures where people do not just work for a paycheck but work for the team. The difference can rest in someone that believed in them enough to give them a chance.

Real-World Example

At a technology company, a new hire arrived with little hands-on software experience. They were quiet in meetings and cautious in their contributions, but they listened intently, asked thoughtful questions, and showed genuine curiosity. Some managers might have sidelined them, waiting for proof of ability. Instead, the team leader saw potential and gave them responsibility as the point of contact for improving internal processes.

Within six months, that same employee was leading a task force on user feedback integration. They had grown from the newest member of the team into a trusted voice shaping strategy, not because they entered with perfect technical skills, but because someone made space for them to grow. The leader did not just develop an employee. They developed a teammate while impacting a life. In doing so, they created trust, loyalty, and impact that extended far beyond one project.

Business Tip

If you want to build a culture where your people win together and grow together, take a tour of *The Sandlot*:

- Do not judge a teammate on their first day
- Celebrating effort before performance
- Coach with patience and presence, not pressure
- Create an environment where it is safe to ask questions
- Remember that belief from a leader can change a career

Great leaders don't just look for stars. They create them.

Final Thought

The Sandlot is more than a nostalgic baseball movie. It is a blueprint for belonging. It is about what happens when a team chooses inclusion over exclusion, patience over perfection, and encouragement over critique. Scotty Smalls did not become part of the team because of his swing. He became part of the team because someone said, "come and play with us because you belong here."

That lesson is timeless. In business and in life, people thrive when they are trusted before they are proven, and when they are welcomed before they are ready. Great teams are not built by collecting perfect résumés. They are built by creating a culture where people can try, stumble, grow, and eventually shine because others believe in them first.

In the movie, the Great Bambino Babe Ruth reminds Benny in his dream, "heroes get remembered, but legends never die. Follow your heart, kid, and you will never go wrong." Your legacy as a leader will not be measured only in deals closed or goals hit. It will be measured in the people you welcomed, mentored, and empowered to carry your culture forward.

Create your own sandlot. Make space for those still finding their swing. Invite them before they are ready. One day, when they tell the story of their career, it won't just be about the work they did. It will be about how you gave them a place on the team and how that made all the difference.

⚾ Section 5: Legacy ⚾

41

The Perfect Pitch – Communicate with Intention

Specificity Wins When the Stakes Are High

Baseball Principle

The perfect pitch is not always about velocity. It is about intention. Nolan Ryan is the all-time leader with 5,714 strikeouts, but what made him legendary was knowing when to unleash that fastball with purpose. Known as The Ryan Express, he mastered the art of throwing a pitch that not only beat the batter but sent a message that this is my game and my moment.

Randy Johnson was equally intimidating standing at 6-foot-10. He is in the second spot behind Ryan with 4,875 lifetime strikeouts. Johnson's greatness was not just in the nastiness of his pitch. It was when he chose to unleash it. The lefty had a slider that buckled knees and broke spirits. Facing the best hitters in the biggest games, he didn't waste pitches. He delivered with precision and confidence. He understood that the right pitch, at the right moment, could end an inning, swing his team's momentum in a game, or decide a championship.

The perfect pitch is not about throwing the fastest ball every time. It is about throwing the right pitch at the right time. It is specificity under pressure, confidence in execution, and communication without words. It's a statement that says, "I know what matters most right now, and I am delivering it."

Business Strategy

Your output in the office is probably not measured in miles per hour, but in relevance and timing. Leaders often believe that the flashier the message, the more impact it will have. This is the business version of just throwing it harder. Like Nolan Ryan and Randy Johnson demonstrated with their fastballs, effectiveness comes not from brute force, but from precision.

An effective speech is won by knowing your audience, reading the room, and delivering exactly what matters most in that moment. It is not about flooding the room with every statistic, every service, or every credential along with your life's story. That is equivalent to throwing wild fastballs out of the zone praying for a called strike.

The winning pitch is clear, intentional, and relevant. It shows you understand the other side's needs, respects their perspective, and offers the solution with confidence. When you deliver that kind of pitch, you do more than hold attention, you earn trust.

Honest intentions earn trust. Relevance earns respect. Just like a perfectly placed fastball or a devastating slider, the right message, at the right moment, can change the entire game.

Real-World Example

When a technology startup sought a partnership with a city's electric authority, the stakes could not have been higher. They were a small team competing against established industry giants, and they had just five minutes on the agenda to make their case.

The CEO could have fallen into the trap of reciting investor stats, technical jargon, or a laundry list of product features. Instead, they chose precision over volume and walked to the podium and began with a single, focused statement.

You're losing nearly 12 percent of grid efficiency each month because of outdated transformer monitoring. Our smart sensors helped Gainesville Regional Utilities reduce energy loss by 37 percent and detect outages two hours faster. We can deliver the same results here and can be up and running in under 90 days.

In one sentence, they reframed the entire conversation. They identified the authority's most pressing pain point, demonstrated credibility with data, and offered a clear timeline for impact. The room leaned in. Questions shifted from skepticism to possibility.

By the end of the month, the city awarded the startup firm the contract. Not because the presentation was flashy, but because it was focused, intentional, and impossible to ignore. That is the perfect pitch in action, measured, meaningful, and timed to win.

Business Tip

To throw the perfect pitch into your professional interactions:

- Research who they are, what they value, and what they are up against
- Tie your message directly to their needs or goals
- Highlight the results you create, not just the work you do
- Rehearse to be clear, concise, and confident without sounding rehearsed
- End with the next step, not a vague impression

Making a presentation, and throwing your pitch, is not just for sales. It is for leadership, influence, and making the connection every time you speak.

Final Thought

There is a pause before every pitch in baseball when everything else fades away. The roar of the crowd, the pressure of the scoreboard, even the weight of expectation all shrinks to a single moment of calmness. Then being poised to deliver with precision. Or framed in another way, it's the space between the notes that makes the music. If there were no space separating the notes, it would just be constant noise.

Nolan Ryan did not intimidate hitters simply because he threw hard. He earned respect because he knew when to unleash the fastball and when to change speeds, making his performance a sweet melody. Randy Johnson terrified batters not only with velocity but with placement, the slider that started at the hip and broke across the plate at the perfect moment like a maestro. Their dominance came not from throwing every pitch with maximum force, but from choosing the right pitch with purpose.

Your words carry the same weight within your own team. The perfect pitch is not about volume, length, or speed. It is about creating a simple symphony. It lands because it is intentional, because it is rooted in empathy and preparation, and because it speaks directly to what matters most in that moment.

When you pause before you speak, you hold the power to shift the outcome. To cut through noise. To show you understand. Like Ryan and Johnson, you do not need to throw everything you have, just the right thing at the right time. Because in the end, the perfect pitch does more than impress. It earns trust. It earns belief and it changes the game.

42

Field the Tough Questions – Crisis Communications & Control

Leadership Is Earned in the Moments That Test You

Baseball Principle

Baseball is a game full of routine plays, of course, until it isn't. Some balls take clean hops and settle gently into the glove. Others test every ounce of focus a fielder has. In the 2001 American League Division Series, Derek Jeter delivered one of the most famous defensive plays in postseason history, known simply as The Flip.

With the Yankees clinging to a one-run lead against the Oakland A's, a ball was hit deep into right field. As the relay throw came in offline, the runner rounded third, and the stadium gasped. It should have been chaos, but Jeter, reading the moment before anyone else, sprinted across the diamond, intercepted the errant throw, and flipped it barehanded to home plate to nail the runner. The play saved the game and kept the Yankees alive.

What made the moment legendary was not just Jeter's athleticism, but his presence. He did not panic at the miscue. He trusted his instincts, anticipated what could go wrong, and executed with total composure when it did.

That is the essence of performing in a crisis. The toughest plays come when everything speeds up, the noise swells, and the stakes skyrocket. The great ones don't freeze. They find stillness inside chaos, they trust their preparation, and act with confidence when everyone else is holding their breath.

Business Strategy

In the professional world, pressure does not send an invitation, it shows up unannounced like a wicked hop. A reporter asks a pointed question in a live on-air interview. A client raises an uncomfortable issue in front of the board. A customer complaint explodes online and gains traction before you even finish your morning coffee.

In those moments, leadership is not defined by how polished you have your script. It is defined by how grounded you are when the script no longer applies. The difference is clear. A reactive leader scrambles, spins, or blames. A prepared leader steadies the room, restores perspective, and earns trust in real time.

Crisis communication is not about covering tracks. It is about setting direction. It requires the discipline to listen first, to acknowledge openly, and to own responsibility when needed. It requires the ability to share facts clearly, manage tone deliberately, and guide everyone back to purpose. When the unexpected hits, the leaders who succeed are not the ones with the fanciest language, they are the ones with the most reliable and honest compass.

Real-World Example

When a state agency experienced a data breach that disrupted critical public services, panic spread quickly inside and outside the agency. Internally, some leaders stayed silent, hoping the issue would fade. Others scrambled to assign blame. Confidence was slipping away by the hour.

The chief communications officer stepped forward. At the press conference, they did not hide behind jargon or scripted evasions. Instead, they began with three simple sentences:
"Here is what we know. Here is what we are doing. Here is what you can expect from us next."

Their direct clarity was disarming. Their honesty was refreshing. The calm tone reframed the entire conversation. What had begun as anger and fear shifted into cautious confidence. The breach was still serious, but the public felt reassured that someone was leading with transparency and control. The department weathered the storm, not because the problem vanished, but because trust held steady.

Business Tip

When fielding tough questions in high-stakes situations, use this four-part playbook:

- Expect hard questions and prepare your responses through scenario mapping and message alignment
- Own the issue honestly and avoid minimizing or shifting blame
- Share the immediate next steps with clarity, not vagueness
- Reinforce your values, purpose, and long-term commitment to rebuilding trust

Control the message not with spin, but with steadiness.

Final Thought

When a ground ball takes a gnarly hop and the stadium gasps, the fielder has no chance to call timeout or replay the moment. The only option is to stay low, keep their eyes on the ball, and trust the preparation that got them there. Fans rarely remember the easy plays. They do remember the ones that tested a player's courage, composure, and commitment under fire.

Leadership under pressure works the same way. The toughest questions come when the tragedy that appears without warning and the headlines that demand a response. These are the bad bounces of business and life. You cannot control their timing, their trajectory, or their speed. What you can control is your presence. Do you flinch, freeze, or lash out? Or do you steady yourself, square up, and make the throw that keeps your team in the game?

Your team, clients, and audience are watching in those moments. In addition to your clients, partners, and the public. They are not measuring the crisis. They are measuring you. They are looking for reassurance that someone is calm in the chaos, prepared in the pressure, and courageous enough to carry the moment.

In the end, your legacy as a leader will not be written by the easy innings. It will be written by how you carried yourself when the game shifted, the ball bounced high, and everyone else held their breath. Bad hops are inevitable. What defines you is the confidence you give others that you can still make the play.

43

Tell the Story, Not Only the Stats – Narrative-Driven Public Relations

Turning Data into Meaning with Human-Centered Brand Narratives

Baseball Principle

Baseball is often described as a game of numbers, batting averages, earned run averages, launch angles, and exit velocity. Ask any fan what they remember most, and it is rarely the stat line. It is the moment. It is Babe Ruth calling his home run shot in Game 3 of the 1932 World Series. It is Hank Aaron breaking Babe Ruth's home run record as some of the crowd poured onto the field in celebration. It is Jackie Robinson stealing home in the 1955 World Series, much to the ire of Yankees catcher Yogi Berra, reminding us that courage can shift history.

The numbers matter, but the moments live forever because they carry meaning. A .300 average is impressive, but it pales in comparison to the story of a kid from Puerto Rico making their major league debut who sent a walk-off home run into the night on Roberto Clemente Day, carrying his family's and country's pride with him around the bases. A 1.88 ERA tells us dominance, but what stirs the heart is the pitcher who struck out the side with the tying run on third, two days after welcoming his first child into the world.

No one understood this balance of fact and feeling better than Vin Scully, the legendary Hall of Fame voice of the Brooklyn and Los Angeles Dodgers for nearly seven decades. Scully never simply announced plays he saw on the field. He invited you into them. He truly painted the green of the grass, enhanced the sound of the crack of the bat, and described the nervous look in a rookie's eyes. He told you where the player came from, what they had overcome, and why the moment mattered. Fans trusted Scully not because of the numbers he recited, but because of the humanity he revealed. Vin Scully proved great communicators know the numbers tell you what happened, but stories tell you why it mattered.

Business Strategy

All business schools train their students to lead with the analytics. They are safe, measurable, and easy to defend. They fill slide decks and board packets with numerical authority. Just like in baseball, numbers alone rarely move people.

A thousand impressions sound important, until you explain what those impressions meant. A 10 percent engagement bump looks good on a chart, but it becomes powerful when you connect it to a story of an employee who felt seen, a customer who felt valued, or a community that acted because of it.

Great communicators understand that while data informs, stories transform. Numbers are headlines. Stories are the heartbeat. A chart can show that your message went viral, but only a narrative can help people feel why it mattered.

When you embed data inside a story, you transform analytics into advocacy. You turn results into relevance. You give your audience something stronger than information, you give them meaning.

Real-World Example

A community theater board was preparing its annual report for donors and stakeholders. The draft presentation was full of strong numbers including ticket sales, sponsorships, contributions, and volunteer hours. The data showed success, but it didn't move anyone. It did not connect because it lacked heart and soul.

The team decided to change the opening. Instead of leading with spreadsheets, they shared a short video about a shy high school student who had joined the youth program. Through rehearsals and performances, that student discovered confidence, found a voice, and eventually earned a college scholarship in the arts. Their parents described how the theater had given their child not just a stage, but a future.

When the numbers came afterward, they landed differently. Stakeholders no longer saw attendance figures. They saw lives transformed, families strengthened, and a community enriched. The theater wasn't just producing performance arts. It was producing possibilities.

Business Tip

To turn data into a compelling story, use the Story Arc Formula across your communication platforms:

- Begin with a human face or relatable situation that grounds the narrative
- Identify the challenge or obstacle and why it mattered
- Show the action taken and what your organization did to help
- Connect the result back to your mission, purpose, or value

People care about a story before they count the numbers. Give them a reason to feel before you ask them to measure.

Final Thought

When Vin Scully stepped into the broadcast booth, he knew his job was never just to read the stat line. Any broadcaster could tell you the count and the score. What made Scully great was that he made the game breathe and come alive. He described the hum of the crowd, the sunlight on the outfield grass, the way a batter stepped out to compose himself before a pitch. He told stories that made players human, and in doing so, he made generations of fans care.

Leaders have the same opportunity. Your audience can find the numbers in a report or a digital dashboard. What they cannot find, unless you give it to them, is the story of why the numbers matter. Tell them about the small business that survived because of a legislative policy change. Share the story of a student who stood taller because of your program. Talk about the family that found hope where they once felt only fear. Make the story personal.

In the end, no one frames a spreadsheet on their wall. They frame the picture of the moment that mattered. They keep the story that gave them pride, joy, or meaning. Just like Vin Scully showed us night after night, the true magic is never in the stats. It is in the story. Here is his call of the historic Kirk Gibson home run in the 1988 World Series, "High fly ball into right field, she is… gone! In a year that has been so improbable, the impossible has happened."

Baseball fans remember those impossible moments, not the math. They may glance at the box score, but what stays with them is the roar of the crowd when the ball clears the fence or the silence before a pitcher delivers a perfect strike. The memory lives in the story.

Your audience is no different. They are not inspired by spreadsheets or statistics. They are moved by purpose, emotion, and authenticity. They want to believe not just in what you do, but in why you do it along with the people who make it possible. So, go beyond the numbers. Tell the story behind success. Show them the human heartbeat behind the data, the faces behind the figures, the impact behind the effort.

Because in the end, no one frames a budget. They frame the moments that meant something, the swing that changed the game, the celebration that united a team, the smile that proved it was all worth it. Those are the stories that last. Those are the stories that make your legacy real.

44

Know Who is Calling Balls and Strikes – Ethics, Compliance, & Media

Understanding Oversight, Standards, and Timing in a Transparent Era

Baseball Principle

Every pitch in baseball is judged by one person, the umpire. The pitcher may stare in disbelief, the batter might shake their head, and the crowd may boo but the umpire's call defines the moment. Their role is not to be liked. It is to be fair and consistent. They are the standard-bearers of fairness, even when the strike zone is debated from the dugout to the broadcast booth, and in the bleacher seats.

Pitchers may think they are in total control, but every throw is filtered through the eyes of the umpire. What looks like a perfect strike to the pitcher may be judged otherwise, and that judgment shapes the outcome of the game. The same principle applies in business and leadership. No decision, announcement, or policy exists in isolation.

Few umpires embodied this responsibility more than Joe West. Credited with umpiring the most games in history with 5,460, West became one of the most recognizable and polarizing figures in Major League Baseball. He was known for his confidence, his longevity, and his insistence that his call was final. Players knew what kind of zone he called. Love him or not, you had to adapt.

The best players did not waste time arguing. They studied the umpire's tendencies, adjusted accordingly, and focused on execution. Whether it was Joe West or Rocky Roe calling balls and strikes, one thing was always true that the game moved forward based on someone's judgment. Games are won by your team's ability to adapt to it.

Business Strategy

Every leader in their business has umpires in regulators, compliance officers, ethics boards, advocacy groups, investors, the press, and even the court of public opinion on social media. These are the ones who decide whether your message lands as fair or foul, credible or questionable. The mistake leaders often make is believing they are pitching into an empty field. Someone is always watching, interpreting, and calling the play.

That is why ethics and timing are inseparable from communication. You may have a brilliant idea, a groundbreaking product, or a carefully worded message. However, if it is delivered without awareness of oversight, accountability, and timing, the brilliance gets overshadowed by the backlash. The best leaders understand that transparency is not a burden. It is a strategic advantage. By anticipating who is calling balls and strikes, you can better align your actions with the standards that earn trust and win the long game.

Real-World Example

A pharmaceutical company prepared to launch a new digital platform designed to streamline customer access and save time. Internally, the project was seen as a major win. The budget was approved, the technology tested, and the marketing materials polished. Leadership envisioned headlines celebrating innovation and forward-thinking service.

Outside their walls, the industry was facing scrutiny. Lawmakers, advocates, and watchdogs were criticizing similar companies for opaque practices and insufficient consumer protections. The timing could not have been more delicate.

Unaware of the storm around them, the organization moved ahead with its planned rollout. Instead of applause, the launch drew skepticism. Headlines framed the announcement not as innovation, but as misdirection, an attempt to shift attention away from broader industry shortcomings. What could have been a showcase of progress became an Strategy of poor judgment and tone-deaf leadership.

Had the organization paused to read the climate, they could have reframed the rollout to acknowledge concerns, highlight safeguards, and position the tool as part of the solution. A slight shift in timing and messaging would have turned liability into leadership. Instead, by ignoring who was calling balls and strikes, they lost the chance to control the narrative and eroded trust they had spent years building.

Business Tip

Use this ethical awareness and timing checklist before any major decision, launch, or announcement:

- Scan headlines, public opinion, and industry news by seeing what else is happening that could color your message
- Identify who holds influence over your space including regulators, compliance teams, industry groups, watchdog organizations, and media voices
- Are you operating within legal, ethical, and cultural expectations by asking if your message reflects your values and the moment
- Ask if the timing, tone, and intent of your communication will land well in the current environment because not every day is the right day to swing.

In today's climate, timing is not a luxury. It is a critically essential responsibility.

Final Thought

Joe West became one of the most recognizable umpires not because players always liked his calls, but because he reminded everyone on the field the reality they could not escape. Someone is always watching, judging, and holding the game accountable. His strike zone was not always perfect, but it was consistent enough that players knew they had to adjust. Those who adapted stayed composed and found ways to win. Those who resisted, arguing every pitch, often lost focus, and the game moved on without them.

Leadership is played under the same conditions across multiple industries. Every decision you make, every statement you make, every action you take is observed by someone who holds influence. Regulators may weigh compliance, clients may evaluate professionalism, the public may scrutinize tone, and your team may measure whether your actions align with your words. You cannot control the calls that come your way, but you can control how you respond to them.

The best leaders do not waste energy fighting every judgment. They recognize that oversight is not the enemy, it is part of the system that gives the game structure and credibility. They know that scrutiny can be uncomfortable, but it is also the proving ground of trust. When you show steadiness under pressure, humility in the face of critique, and integrity when the easy path would be to spin or deflect, you earn something far more valuable than a favorable call. You earn belief.

Your legacy will not be measured by the days when everything went smoothly. It will be defined by the moments when your team was behind in the bottom of the ninth inning, the crowd was restless, and the outcome depended on how you carried yourself when the strike zone seemed to shrink. Consistency builds credibility. That credibility builds trust and in today's world, trust is the only score that matters.

45

Read the Situation Before You Steal – Briefings & Message Discipline

Staying on Message, Respecting the Strategy, and Avoiding Unforced Errors

Baseball Principle

Stealing a base is never just about raw speed. It is a chess match played in split seconds. The legacy of great base stealers like Rickey Henderson, Lou Brock, and Vince Coleman turned it into an art form. They studied the pitcher's every twitch, the catcher's arm strength, and the count on the batter. No matter how much instinct they had, they still relied on one critical factor, getting the go signal from the situation in front of them.

Go too soon by leaning towards second and you risk being picked off. Go without the sign and you might distract the batter or derail the inning. The stolen base is electrifying when it works, but it is disastrous when done recklessly.

The best base stealers were not gamblers. They were disciplined opportunists who blended instinct with intelligence, daring with discipline, and always with trust in the strategy. They knew that the steal was not about showing off speed, it was about advancing the team's bigger game plan.

Business Strategy

The pressure to move quickly, especially when the spotlight is on, can tempt even the best leaders to act without alignment. A CEO rushes through a speech at a trade group before reviewing the team's talking points. A manager shares preliminary data that later changes. An enthusiastic employee posts on social media before the campaign is ready. Each one feels like a small step forward, but without coordination, it can create confusion, damage credibility, or even derail momentum.

Briefings that create team cohesion are not bureaucracy, they are protection. They are the signals that keep everyone in sync, ensuring that what is said publicly matches the strategy worked out privately. They prevent mixed messages, avoid unnecessary corrections, and protect the trust your audience has in you.

The most effective leaders know that communication is not just about quick response, it is about precision. They respect the process, align with the plan, and wait for the sign based on game around them. When they do move, the impact is amplified because the timing, message, and team are all working together.

Real-World Example

In a small town, the city council was preparing to announce a new downtown revitalization plan. The mayor, city manager, and planning director had worked together on a coordinated rollout with clear messaging, a shared timeline, and supporting visuals. However, before the official launch, one well-meaning council member gave an ill-advised interview with the local paper. They used outdated numbers and spoke off script, making promises that were not part of the plan.

Residents were confused. Business owners worried about changes that were never intended. Instead of excitement, the town had to spend days clarifying and correcting the story. The initial excitement of the plan was diminished.

For their next major announcement, the city council adopted a simple rule that no one spoke to the press or community groups without a quick internal pre-briefing to align on key points. That small change paid off because of one negative experience with the rouge but well-intentioned Councilmember. Every official now committed to sharing the same vision as a team. Reporters and the community received accurate details. Citizens felt confident because the message came through clear and united.

Business Tip

Use this pre-communication checklist to ensure message discipline:

- Never assume you are aligned, with a quick check-in can prevent major missteps
- Know the top three takeaways your audience needs to hear
- Understand sensitive topics, evolving issues, or timing restrictions
- Know who else is speaking and how their message fits with yours
- Ask if now the right time is to speak, or if patience will serve the message better

Message discipline builds message power. Respect the process to protect the outcome.

Final Thought

The greatest base stealers in baseball did achieve success by simply being fast. Rickey Henderson studied the pitcher's pick off move, trusted the strategy, and only ran when the situation confirmed the timing was right. The sign from the third base coach was more than a green light because the game dynamics dictated it was the right call. That is why his daring steals became legendary rather than reckless.

Leadership works the same way. Moving quickly feels bold, but speed without alignment creates risk. A message rushed to the press, a social post sent too soon, a decision made without input, each can throw off the rhythm of your entire team. The problem is not ambition. It is acting outside the plan.

The leaders who win consistently are the ones who blend urgency with discipline. They respect the process, honor the people behind it, and know that waiting for the right situation is not weakness, it is wisdom.

The next time you feel the urge to sprint ahead, call time out. Check in. Make sure the timing is right. Because in both baseball and business, the success of the steal is not just in the speed of the sprint, it is in the trust that everyone is moving together with the same strategy. Do not get thrown out trying to impress with vanity metrics. Get the sign, read the game situation, and then take your lead and run with it.

46

Own the Postgame – Marketing Reporting & Relationship Building

Turning Performance into Partnership with Honest and Trusted Follow-Through

Baseball Principle

The game may be decided by the final out, but sometimes the future is shaped in the postgame. Reflection in the clubhouse is where raw results become lessons. In the agony of defeat, emotions can be channeled into resolve. Teams can decide whether setbacks will break them or build them. Will the losses bring them together to achieve victory as a solid unit the next game day.

No story captures this better than the 2004 Boston Red Sox. Down three games against the New York Yankees in the American League Championship Series, Boston stood on the edge of elimination. Most teams would have unraveled. Instead, the Red Sox owned their postgame moments. Their meetings after each painful loss weren't filled with blame, they were built on belief, honesty, and accountability.

Johnny Damon embodied that spirit. His energy, grit, and relentless positivity became a lifeline for the 2004 Red Sox when the weight of history pressed hard against them. Both in the dugout and clubhouse, Damon refused to let frustration take hold. He redirected conversations away from doubt and toward action, focusing teammates on the next step and the response required. That constant reframing kept the team from tightening under pressure. His presence anchored the clubhouse, creating the belief and looseness that allowed them to play their best baseball in the most defining moments of their season.

With the comeback nearly complete with the series all tied up at three, the payoff came in Game 7 of the American League Championship Series. Damon delivered one of the most defining performances of his career and Boston sports history with two home runs, including a grand slam, that silenced Yankee Stadium and completed the greatest playoff comeback in baseball history. The Red Sox carried that resilience into the World Series, winning over the St. Louis Cardinals and breaking the 86-year Curse of the Bambino, the belief that Boston was doomed after selling Babe Ruth to the Yankees in 1919.

The championship celebration was euphoric, and the curse was officially shattered. It was the postgame culture, fueled by leaders like Damon. Truth was spoken, trust was built, and resilience was renewed, that made the miracle possible.

Business Strategy

In marketing, public relations, or any client-focused work, the campaign itself may feel like the main event, but the real relationship is built after the final ads run or the press coverage fades. The debrief is your postgame. It is where performance turns into trust.

Too often, teams fall into the trap of presenting only glossy headlines or flashy metrics. That might win applause in the moment, but it does little to strengthen a long-term partnership. True credibility comes from honest reporting, thoughtful analysis, and a willingness to admit where adjustments are needed.

Clients do not just want to hear what went right. They want to know what you discovered. They want to see that you are already thinking about how to make the next campaign sharper, smarter, and more effective. That is how you turn a one-time project into an ongoing collaboration. By proving that every postgame is not about defending the past but about preparing for the future together.

Real-World Example

A health care network partnered with a communications firm to execute a multi-state campaign promoting preventive screenings. The campaign included paid media, community outreach, patient testimonials, and physician engagement. The launch was smooth and early results showed promise, but what cemented the relationship was what happened after the rollout.

Instead of a one-sided report, the firm coordinated a comprehensive post-campaign summit. They brought together representatives from every region, presented clear but honest metrics side by side with patient impact stories, and facilitated breakout discussions on lessons learned. They did not just talk about KPIs (key performance indicators), they talked about barriers, successes, and what it meant for underserved communities reached for the first time.

The firm also identified areas of underperformance and proactively offered solutions, not excuses. They showed how feedback had already been integrated into planning for the next phase. The meeting ended not with applause, but with alignment. That approach turned a transactional project into a long-term, trust-based partnership. The client saw the agency not as a vendor, but as an extension of their mission.

Business Tip

Make every post-campaign debrief a strategic opportunity by following this framework:

- Translate data into insights by stating what the performance means
- Invite clients to share their perspective before offering your own
- Owning weaknesses earns more respect than hiding them
- Tie results to long-term objectives, not just immediate outputs
- Use the report as a springboard for the next initiative

A report should not feel like a final exam. It should feel like the first meeting of what comes next.

Final Thought

The 2004 Red Sox did not make history because they ignored their losses. They owned them. After each game, the clubhouse became a place of recalibration, where details were dissected, belief was reinforced, and resolve was renewed. Johnny Damon, the two-time MLB All-Star and two-time World Series Champion, was at the heart of that team culture. He reminded his teammates that the next at-bat, the next inning, the next game could flip the entire story. When the moment came in Game 7, it was Damon who delivered the exclamation point, with his grand slam, that completed the greatest comeback in baseball history. His story even earned him a co-starring role in the movie *Fever Pitch* with Drew Barrymore and Jimmy Fallon recounting the Red Sox historic victory.

Business works the same way. Clients and colleagues are not only watching the game, the campaign, the presentation, or the launch. They are also watching what happens after. Some leaders rush past the lessons and move on too quickly. Stronger leaders stop to reflect, study, and apply what they learned. Reporting is not a chore but a chance to build credibility and trust.

Postgame reflection is not paperwork. It is partnership. It is the moment when you prove that you are not just delivering results, you are invested in the long game. The postgame is where reputations are strengthened, trust is deepened, and future opportunities are earned.

Do not just celebrate the win and move on. Open the notebook. Study the film. Invite honest dialogue. Because when you own the postgame, like Johnny Damon and the 2004 Red Sox, you transform results into resilience, clients into partners, and good work into legacy. Own the postgame, and you will always get the chance to step up to the plate again.

47

Play the Long Season, Not the Inning – Communication Consistency

Building Trust and Momentum Through Steady, Sustained Effort

Baseball Principle

Momentum can shift in the blink of an eye. One inning you are cruising with a three-run lead, the next you are scrambling after a bloop single, a defensive error, and a questionable call. Fans can feel these game momentums shift intensely, but players and managers know something critical. A single game, or even a losing streak, rarely defines a season. Over 162 games, consistency outweighs chaos.

The 2025 Cleveland Guardians proved that truth. At one point in mid-season after falling into a brutal slump they were 15½ games behind the division leading Detroit Tigers in the American League Central. During that stretch they endured a 10-game losing streak, marking the club's first double-digit skid since 2012. Many teams in that situation would have panicked, made wild roster moves, chased short-term fixes, and reshuffled lineups. The Guardians instead held their ground. Manager Stephen□Vogt urged patience and resilience, emphasizing keeping faith in the process even still being 11 games out of first place on September 4. They trusted their talent, stuck to their game plan, made steady adjustments, and kept grinding. That quiet, persistent mindset not only carried them out of the hole, but all the way past Detroit and into winning the AL Central, the largest comeback in MLB history.

Baseball history is full of cautionary tales of managers who overreact, burning out pitchers by chasing every short-term edge, pulling sluggers out of slumps with constant tinkering, or disrupting chemistry with rash roster moves. The most successful teams, by contrast, recognize that greatness is earned over months of repetition, trust, and composure. They know that one inning, one game, even one losing streak is just a snapshot, not the whole season.

The lesson is clear. The teams that win over time are the teams that resist panic, embrace patience, and keep executing their plan day after day.

Business Strategy

A single quarter's numbers, a campaign's metrics, or even one client's reaction can feel monumental, but they are only snapshots in a much larger season. Too many leaders make the mistake of overreacting to short-term fluctuations. They react by canceling a campaign after a slow month, shifting brand messages so frequently that customers never have time to connect, or rebranding every year in search of a quick win. Those moves create noise, not loyalty.

Consistency is not stubbornness, but strategic discipline. It means knowing what your brand stands for, staying committed to that core identity, and making purposeful adjustments without losing your foundation. Imagine a company that changes its logo, slogan, and tone every year. Customers would never know who they are dealing with. Contrast that with Coca-Cola, which has updated its visuals countless times but never strayed from its timeless promise of refreshment and togetherness with their iconic look. The styles evolved, but the story remained steady.

The same applies to your work. Communication consistency is the quiet force that builds recognition, trust, and authority over time. Clients, customers, and colleagues do not just notice what you say once, they notice what you repeat with conviction, year after year. The organizations that win are not those chasing every short-term reaction, but those that keep showing up with the same clear voice, steady presence, and long-term commitment.

Real-World Example

An entrepreneur launched a gourmet food truck with big expectations. The first month brought mixed results, some nights the lines were long, other days the truck sat quiet. Friends and even a few investors suggested pivoting fast including changing the menu, rebranding the truck, or chasing every new food trend. Instead, the owner chose consistency. The truck kept its core identity, signature dishes, bright branding, and a message built around community and quality. Adjustments were made thoughtfully. Parking in higher-traffic spots at events, posting more consistently on social media, and building a loyalty program for repeat customers.

By the end of the year, what once seemed like a struggling idea had become a staple. People began recognizing the truck by name, looking forward to its weekly stops, and recommending it to friends. The steady branding and consistent presence, built trust, and trust built a following.

If the owner had judged success by the first few months alone, the business would have disappeared before customers ever had a chance to connect. By playing the long season, the food truck grew from a risky startup into a community favorite.

Business Tip

Resist the temptation to overhaul your campaign at the first sign of slow results.

- Anticipate the ramp-up, the in-game adjustments, and the push toward your final goals
- Short-term metrics should inform tweaks, not dictate complete overhauls
- Keep your core tone, visuals, and narrative intact to build recognition and trust
- Adjust improve performance without losing sight of the larger vision
- Constant resets drain focus and enthusiasm, as stability fuels creativity and execution

Do not abandon your strategy at the first dip in numbers as consistency builds trust. Use short-term results to refine, not to reinvent, and keep your core message steady for lasting impact.

Final Thought

Every team will face innings where nothing seems to fall their way. The bats go cold, the errors pile up, and the scoreboard looks unforgiving. The championship teams understand that a season is not defined by one bad stretch, it is defined by resilience, trust, and the discipline to stick with a plan built for the long haul. They know momentum is fragile, but identity is strong.

The same truth holds in offices across impacting countless sectors. A slow quarter, a campaign that misses early targets, or a project that stumbles out of the gate does not mean failure. It is a moment that tests whether leaders have the courage to stay steady, the wisdom to adjust without panic, and the vision to keep their people aligned with the larger purpose. Anyone can lead when the scoreboard is in their favor. The real measure comes when patience is tested, and the outcome is uncertain.

The leaders who win are not the ones who tear up the playbook at the first sign of struggle. They are the ones who keep perspective, rally their teams, and stay focused on the destination while weathering the storms of the journey. Over time, their consistency builds confidence, their calm creates stability, and their persistence delivers results.

A rough losing streak is just a chapter, not the whole story. The season is long, and the opportunities will come. Those who refuse to lose sight of the bigger picture are the ones who finish as champions, on the field and in the boardroom. In his second year as serving as manager of Guardians, Stephen Vogt earned his second American League Manager of the Year award in back-to-back seasons because he stayed the course, steadying the ship, and leading the team to an improbable division championship.

48

Double Play Delivery – Solving Two Issues with One Tactic

Maximizing Efficiency and Impact with Strategic Execution

Baseball Principle

AJ Pierzynski of the Chicago White Sox never made it easy on opponents because he was always thinking about ways he could throw his opponents off their game. In fact, a *Men's Journal* MLB survey labeled him the most hated player in baseball. His own manager with Chicago White Sox Ozzie Guillén once said, "When you play against AJ, you hate him, but when he plays for you, you hate him a little less." Pierzynski, an All-Star and World Series Champion, earned that reputation not just because he could hit and call a strong game behind the plate, but because he mastered the art of distraction. Pierzynski had a knack for doing two things at once. He contributed to his own team's success while brilliantly throwing his opponents off balance.

Whether it was a hard slide, a sharp exchange with a batter, Pierzynski found ways to turn one tactic into two outcomes. In the 2005 ALCS, Pierzynski turned a strikeout into a game-changing play when he ran to first on a controversial dropped third strike. Although the catcher signaled for an out, the umpire ruled the ball hit the ground. Pierzynski reached first safely, the White Sox brought in a pinch-runner, and a double followed, setting up the winning run. One moment became two outcomes, and Chicago took control of the series.

Like a perfectly executed double play, Pierzynski's style of play solved two problems at once, he produced results for the White Sox while undermining the focus of his opponents. That is why fans of Chicago loved him, opponents despised him, and teammates respected him. It was not just about raw ability, it was strategy. Pierzynski knew that winning was not only about the scoreboard. It was about controlling the mental game, and if he could disrupt and deliver at the same moment, he gave his team a decisive edge.

Business Strategy

A timely double play is more than just efficient. It is strategic foresight throwing the right pitch with the right batter in the box. It happens when one deliberate action achieves multiple objectives, multiplying results without multiplying effort. The best leaders know that resources, time, and attention are limited. Instead of chasing every goal through separate projects, they design initiatives that serve layered purposes.

Consider any company launching a sustainability program. On the surface, it reduces environmental impact. With the right framing, it also enhances brand reputation, strengthens community partnerships, and attracts younger talent who want to work for a value-driven organization. One strategic initiative, several wins for the organization.

Next consider the CEO's corporate town hall address. A less strategic leader might treat it as a single communication, share updates, answer questions, move on. A smarter leader views it as a chance to align strategy, boost morale, clarify expectations, and showcase authenticity in one moment. The message is sharper, the delivery intentional, and the outcomes exponential.

Too often, organizations fall into silos. Marketing pushes awareness. Compliance checks boxes for policy regulations. Human Resources drives culture. Operations pursue efficiency. Each one moves separately, like fielders who do not talk to each other. But when leadership connects the dots, when departments and initiatives are aligned, every move begins to produce compounded value and multiple team victories.

Real-World Example

A regional bank faced two pressing challenges. First, it needed to boost adoption of its new mobile banking app, which promised customers easier deposits, bill pay, and transfers. At the same time, the bank was still working to repair its reputation after negative headlines about fees and long customer service waiting times.

Rather than treat these as separate initiatives, the bank combined the goals into one strategy. It launched a Banking Made Personal roadshow, sending branch managers and digital specialists into community events, small business forums, and college campuses. At each stop, staff walked customers through the app's features in real time while also holding open conversations about fees, account services, and long-standing concerns while signing up new account holders.

The impact was immediate. Customers began adopting the app with confidence, not only because of the technology itself but because they learned about it directly from people they trusted. Just as importantly, the bank's leadership demonstrated accountability by showing up, listening, and addressing questions face-to-face. Media outlets and local influencers began covering the events, reframing the bank's story as one of transparency, modernization, and genuine community engagement.

With one carefully crafted initiative, the bank solved two major problems, driving technology adoption and rebuilding credibility. That is what a double play looks like in business with one action, two wins, and momentum shifting firmly in the right direction.

Business Tip

To deliver a double play that drives real results:

- Identify objectives that can share strategic alignment and timelines
- Build campaigns or messages that intentionally serve more than one need
- Maximize impact by distributing the effort across multiple platforms
- Find areas where a single solution can resolve friction between priorities
- After the play, assess what worked for each objective and refine your approach

A great double play is not improvised. It is anticipated, designed, and executed with unity and precision.

Final Thought

The power of the double play is not just in the out, it is in the orchestration. It is a moment when timing, trust, and plans align to deliver exponential value. Great teams do not chase efficiency for their own sake. They design it into their strategy.

AJ Pierzynski understood that better than most. His game was never about one move alone. A base hit was also a chance to rattle a pitcher. A hard tag was also a statement of toughness. Pierzynski, reaching first base on a dropped third strike, was about creating chaos that changed the series. He found ways to turn a single action into multiple outcomes, producing on the field while disrupting his opponents. He knew that momentum could be shifted not just by performance, but by cunning design.

The same principle applies in many organizational operations. When you stop seeing goals as isolated tasks and start viewing them as opportunities for alignment, you unlock momentum. One campaign can build awareness and rebuild trust. One message can set expectations and inspire loyalty. One strategic move can solve two problems at once and position you for the next win.

Do not aim to check boxes. Aim to connect them. Look for the play that turns defense into offense. Recognize the pitch. Anticipate the move. Then make the throw that solves two problems with one motion. That is not luck. That is leadership by design. Just as it was for Pierzynski and the World Series Champion White Sox, it is how great teams win the long game.

49

Respect the Rain Delay – Navigating External Disruption

Leading with Patience, Perspective, and Preparation When Plans Get Washed Out

Baseball Principle

Rain delays evaluate more than the stadium grounds crew, they assess a team's patience, focus, and preparation. No matter how ready a team is, how perfect the lineup looks, or how loud the crowd roars, when the skies open and the rain pours down, everything stops. The tarp covers the infield, players disappear into the clubhouse, and thousands of fans wait, hoping the storm will pass.

One of the most famous examples came in 2011, when the Tampa Bay Rays and the Minnesota Twins endured a five-hour and three-minute rain delay, the longest in Major League history. For players, that meant over five hours of waiting, stretching, keeping loose, and trying not to lose focus before finally taking the field again. Some dug in mentally, preparing for the restart. Others struggled to stay sharp. When play resumed, the difference showed. The Rays, who stayed ready, pulled out the win.

That is the essence of a rain delay, it does not cancel the game, it changes it. Momentum shifts, strategies reset, and the outcome often belongs to the team that treated the delay not as wasted time, but as preparation time. Rain delays remind us that leadership is not about controlling the uncontrollable, it is about how you respond when disruption strikes.

Business Strategy

External disruptions are the modern rain delays. Economic downturns, sudden policy shifts, natural disasters, supply chain breakdowns, and global events can stop momentum in its tracks, no matter how strong your preparation. A new policy can be overshadowed by breaking news. A promising contract can stall when budgets freeze. A carefully built strategy can be reshuffled overnight by a leadership change.

You cannot control these moments, but you can control your response. The best leaders anticipate that storms will come. They design strategies with contingency plans, flexible budgets, and adaptable messaging so they are not caught flat-footed. They prepare their teams to shift gears without panic, keeping morale steady and focus sharp.

Like players waiting through a rain delay, they know the interruption is not the end of the game, it is part of the game. The leaders who thrive are the ones who use the delay to recalibrate, strengthen communication, and prepare for the moment the skies clear. They respect the disruption without surrendering momentum, ensuring their organizations return to the field ready to perform, not just resume.

Real-World Example

A small family-owned café on Florida's Gulf Coast just finished investing in a new marketing push to attract morning commuters and expand its catering services. Flyers were printed, social media ads were scheduled, and a new menu rollout was ready to launch. A powerful hurricane swept through the region, leaving widespread flooding, power outages, and closed roads for months.

Instead of pressing ahead with their campaign as if nothing had changed, the owners shifted focus. They paused their planned promotions and turned their kitchen into a community support hub. Using their remaining inventory, they offered free coffee and simple meals to first responders and neighbors cleaning up storm damage. They posted updates on social media, not about sales, but about resources, safety tips, and encouragement.

When power and stability returned, they relaunched their menu with a new message of "Stronger Together, Fueled Locally." The storm had disrupted their marketing calendar, but it had also given them a chance to demonstrate heart, resilience, and community spirit. As a result, their reputation grew stronger than before, drawing in loyal customers who valued not just their food, but their role as a trusted neighbor.

They respected the rain delay. By responding with patience and purpose, they turned disruption into long-term credibility.

Business Tip

To lead well during external disruption:

- Build margin into your timelines and plans
- Monitor environmental, economic, and social factors that may impact timing
- Pause messaging if it risks appearing insensitive or irrelevant
- Communicate clearly with stakeholders about changes and new expectations
- Use the downtime to refine strategy or conduct internal improvements

A delay is not wasted time. It is a chance to reset, reflect, and prepare for a smarter reentry.

Final Thought

The best teams do not let the weather ruin their three-game home series against an opponent. They know that storms will pass, delays will end, and the true test of character is what happens during the wait. A rain delay is not wasted time, it is a test of preparation, patience, and perspective. Players who sulk lose their edge. Players who stay sharp come back stronger when the tarp comes off the field.

Delays in traditional business are no different. Disruptions will arise in hurricanes, economic downturns, policy changes, or sudden market shifts. You cannot control the skies, but you can control your response. Leaders who panic during the storm often lose the trust of their teams and customers. Leaders who stay calm, protect their reputation, and use the pause to prepare send a clear message that we will be ready when the game resumes.

The rain will come. Delays are inevitable, but what matters is being ready to play when the field clears. The storm is not an excuse but an opportunity to sharpen focus. Frustration does not build momentum, but resilience does. The teams and leaders who embrace the pause, adjust with patience, and return with renewed energy are the ones who turn setbacks into defining victories.

Seasons are not defined by the storms. They are defined by the comeback. The organizations that embrace the delay, stay ready through uncertainty, and lead with patience are the ones that emerge stronger, sharper, and ultimately victorious when the skies finally clear.

50

Win the Fans, Not Just the Game – Brand Loyalty Through Purpose

Building Lasting Connections Through Values That Matter

Baseball Principle

The Savannah Bananas did not begin as an entertainment powerhouse. In fact, they were born out of struggle. When Jesse Cole and his wife Emily took over a failing college summer league baseball franchise in Savannah, Georgia, the team had no money, no fans, and no clear future. Traditional baseball strategy said to focus on winning games, signing better players, and hoping attendance followed. While mortgaging their home to afford their vision, the Coles and the Bananas chose a different path.

They decided their mission was not just baseball. Their mission was entertainment, joy, and community. From dancing players and breakdancing umpires to music videos and fan-first ticketing policies, they turned every game into an experience. Instead of asking, how do we sell more tickets? They asked, how do we make every fan feel like part of something bigger?

The results were staggering. What began as a small-town experiment became an international phenomenon. The Bananas sold out at their local home minor league stadium regularly and then raised the bar. Then they took the show on the road, packing MLB, NFL, and NCAA college football stadiums for multiple nights, routinely outdrawing the stadium's home teams themselves.

The Savannah Bananas proved what many forget that loyalty does not come from the scoreboard. It comes from purpose. Fans do not only show up for wins. They show up for meaning, for joy, for identity, and for a story they want to belong.

Business Strategy

Too many organizations focus on winning transactions but forget to win hearts. They invest heavily in features, efficiencies, or making quarterly numbers, as if loyalty automatically follows. Just like a baseball team that obsesses over stats without energizing its fans, these companies miss the deeper truth. People do not stay loyal because of performance alone. The fans stay loyal because of connection.

The businesses that stand out are the ones that transform everyday interactions into meaningful experiences. They think about how a client feels at every touchpoint. From the first handshake to the follow-up email. They design moments of surprise and delight. They make customers feel seen, valued, and part of a shared journey. Purpose becomes the glue holding everything together. When the story is bigger than the product, loyalty then becomes bigger than the transaction.

Like the Bananas, successful organizations think beyond transactions. They invest in the experience. They focus on delight, surprise, and authentic connections that align their values with the values of their audience. That commitment shows in customer-first philosophies, transparent communication, and bold creativity that transforms a brand into a movement. The companies that win the fans are not always the ones with the sleekest product. They are the ones that make people feel like insiders, like family, like part of something special.

Real-World Example

Imagine a professional services firm rolling out a new client platform. On paper, technology works. The data is accurate. The features are competitive. But adoption lags because clients feel disconnected, it feels like just another tool, not a relationship.

The firm steps back and rethinks its approach. Instead of pushing the product, they build a movement around partnership. They host interactive workshops, highlight client success stories, and make onboarding an experience rather than a task. They talk less about features and more about shared outcomes, growth, trust, progress.

Within months, something shifts. Clients no longer describe themselves as users of a platform. They describe themselves as partners in a mission, becoming fans. Retention rises. Referrals increase. Loyalty deepens, not because of technology alone, but because the firm gave people something to believe in.

Business Tip

To build brand loyalty through purpose:

- Define your core values and communicate them consistently
- Support causes that align with your identity and audience
- Involve your employees and customers in purpose-driven efforts
- Share real stories that connect your mission to community impact
- Make sure your actions match your words at every level of the organization

People remember what you stand for as an organization far longer than what you sell. They will remember how you made them feel.

Final Thought

The Savannah Bananas began in a simple older minor-league ballpark and a bold dream, to reimagine what baseball could mean to people. They were not chasing standings or chasing stars. They were chasing hearts. Today, they sell out stadiums once reserved for the biggest names in sports, not because they always win on the field, but because they always win in the stands. Their goal is not to collect trophies, but to collect one billion fans. Fans who feel joy, belonging, and purpose every time they experience the game.

That is the challenge for you as a leader. Winning the task, the project, or even the quarter will get you attention. Winning the trust, belief, and loyalty of your people will earn you something far greater, allegiance that lasts.

This book has not been about baseball alone. It has been about the deeper lesson baseball teaches us. Your legacy is not measured in numbers, but in the individual lives you touch, the voices that rise with you, and the fans who stay by your side long after the lights go out.

Play for something bigger than yourself because the scoreboard will fade but the fans you win will carry your story forward. In baseball and in business, the true legacy is not in the box score. It is in the hearts of the people who choose to cheer for you, come back to you, and advocate for you even when the game is over. Lead with purpose. Focus on creating an honorable legacy by winning over your fans.

🎬 Movie Break: *Bull Durham* 🎬

Quiet Leadership and Coaching Through Chaos

Baseball Principle

Crash Davis is a career lifer in the minor leagues. He knows the grind, the game, and the mindset it takes to stay relevant over a long season. In *Bull Durham*, he is brought in during the twilight of his playing career as a catcher, not to win games, but to mentor a hot-headed phenom pitcher named Ebby Calvin "Nuke" LaLoosh.

While Nuke throws wild fastballs and daydreams of major league glory, Crash brings perspective. He mentors. He steadies. He sacrifices his own ambition to build someone else's foundation.

Crash is not the star. He is the structure. He is the glue that holds the Durham Bulls clubhouse together, even when he knows his own career is nearing an end while approaching the honorable and yet dubious distinction of being the minor leagues all-time career home run leader.

That is the heartbeat of true leadership. It is not about being the face of the franchise. It is about building the future. It is about speaking truth, delivering hard lessons, and setting the tone when egos flare and tempers rise.

Crash never made it back to the show, but he ends the season eventually setting the minor league home run record with a lower-level minor league team after being released by the Durham Bulls when Nuke was called up to the majors. Crash fulfilled his purpose and walked away with dignity, pride, and a potential future as a big-league manager.

Business Strategy

Crash Davis embodies the leadership traits that do not always come with a title. He is emotionally intelligent, strategically patient, and grounded in purpose. He knows his role and plays it with pride.

Many professionals find themselves in the Crash phase of their career. They have the experience, the wisdom, and the ability to mentor, but they are overlooked in favor of flashy newcomers or trend chasers. The temptation is to become bitter or to check out.

Crash does the opposite. He leans in. He brings out the best in others. He communicates calmly, delivers with precision, and leads with consistency.

In a time when careers shift rapidly and younger voices dominate the room. The Crash Davises of the business world are more valuable than ever. They are the communicators who keep projects on track. They are the advisors who guide without drama. They are the ones who finish strong, even if the spotlight never finds them.

Real-World Example

At a consulting firm, a senior strategist was passed over for a long-anticipated director promotion. It was a blow after years of hard work, long nights, and proven results seemed to fall short. But instead of disengaging, they chose a different response. They focused on mentoring younger consultants, stabilizing client relationships, and quietly rebuilding morale after a turbulent year.

Over time, their steady presence became the glue that held the culture together. They didn't seek the spotlight. They strengthened the system. Three years later, when the company underwent a major restructuring, leadership realized that this strategist's influence had already shaped every department. They were promoted, but not to a title they once chased, but to a role that reflected who they had become as the firm's head of training, culture, and communications.

Their leadership journey didn't climb a straight ladder. It expanded outward, rooted in service and authenticity. Like Crash Davis, they didn't get the call they once expected. They got the opportunity that matched their purpose to teach, to steady, and to lead from the heart.

Business Tip

If you are a seasoned professional navigating uncertain transitions or mentoring younger talent, consider the *Bull Durham* playbook:

- Leadership is not about being boisterous, it is about being consistent
- You can coach without a title, and guide without needing applause
- Experience is valuable only if you use it to uplift others
- Recognize your influence even when your path shifts
- As expressed in the movie, you throw the ball, you hit the ball, and you catch the ball

Set your own journey. Find your next opportunity and teach someone else how to manage the game along the way.

Final Thought

Bull Durham is not really about baseball. It is about the quiet truth of leadership. Crash Davis does not get the glory. He does not ride off into the sunset with a trophy in hand. His career ends in obscurity, a release notice, a duffel bag, and the hum of stadium lights turning off one last time. What he leaves behind is far greater than numbers in a record book.

He leaves a legacy. As Susan Sarandon's character Annie Savoy says in the movie, "you have to respect the ballplayer who just wants to finish the season." And Crash completed the season with respect.

In teaching Nuke how to carry himself, how to handle pressure, how to respect the game. Crash showed what true leaders do, they make others better, even if it costs them their own chance at the spotlight. His gift was not a home run record. It was wisdom. His triumph was not in personal accolades. It was in knowing that the player who came after him was prepared to succeed.

That is the deeper lesson for all of us. Leadership is not about chasing applause. It is about planting seeds that may grow long after you have walked away. It is about choosing impact over attention. It is about leaving your fingerprints on the future through the people you guide, encourage, and prepare for their moment.

You may not always be recognized. You may not always get credit. If you lead with conviction, with clarity, and with commitment to others, your influence will ripple forward in ways you may never see.

Leadership is not measured by what you achieve for yourself. It is measured by what endures in others because of you, as sometimes, the quietest endings write the most meaningful and remembered legacies.

⚾ Grand Slam Leadership Conclusion ⚾

Grand Slam Leadership is not just about baseball. It is about you. The leader, the teammate, the professional who wants to win in business and in life. Baseball gives us the principles, the metaphors, and the memories. What stays with you are the lessons. Patience at the plate, discipline on defense, resilience after an error, and the power of playing for something bigger than yourself.

Just like in the ballpark, your career will bring walk-off wins and crushing strikeouts. You will face the pressure of full counts, the sting of bad hops, and the challenge of leading when the game speeds up. What matters most is not the stat sheet. What matters is how you show up, how you build trust, create belonging, share stories that move people, and steady your team when the spotlight burns brightest.

The legends of the game, from Vin Scully's storytelling to Babe Ruth's called shot to the determination of Johnny Damon and the grand theatrics of Kirk Gibson, remind us that greatness is never about numbers alone. It is about a story with meaning. It is about connection. It is about believing in the mission and in each other. By living a life of purpose with character and faith while loving your family, the game, and mission like Hall of Fame catcher Gary Carter.

As you turn these lessons into action, remember that your legacy will not be measured only in sales, metrics, or quarterly results. It will live in the people you coached, the colleagues you lifted, the culture you created, and the moments you made matter.

Baseball teaches us that heroes are remembered, but the legends will truly never die. The same is true for leaders. Your impact will carry forward in the lives you touched, and the stories others tell about how you made them feel seen, valued, and believed in.

This is your invitation to lead like the game is on the line. To step into the box with confidence, to steady your team when the pressure rises, and to build a legacy that lasts far beyond the season.

In the end, the wins that matter most are not just the ones on the scoreboard. They are the wins you create in the hearts of the people who choose to believe in you, follow you, and play on your team.

Play Ball!

If you would like to contact Dr. Bobby Olszewski please email: **DrBobbyO@EmersonMCG.com**

www.ingramcontent.com/pod-product-compliance
Lightning Source LLC
Chambersburg PA
CBHW032121040426
42449CB00005B/208
9798994343104